Memoirs of a Defense Contractor

Memoirs of a Defense Contractor

T. H. Henning

iUniverse, Inc.
New York Lincoln Shanghai

Memoirs of a Defense Contractor

Copyright © 2005 by Thomas H. Henning

All rights reserved. No part of this book may be used or reproduced by any means, graphic, electronic, or mechanical, including photocopying, recording, taping or by any information storage retrieval system without the written permission of the publisher except in the case of brief quotations embodied in critical articles and reviews.

iUniverse books may be ordered through booksellers or by contacting:

iUniverse
2021 Pine Lake Road, Suite 100
Lincoln, NE 68512
www.iuniverse.com
1-800-Authors (1-800-288-4677)

ISBN-13: 978-0-595-36326-1 (pbk)
ISBN-13: 978-0-595-80762-8 (ebk)
ISBN-10: 0-595-36326-1 (pbk)
ISBN-10: 0-595-80762-3 (ebk)

Printed in the United States of America

Contents

Preface xi

CHAPTER 1   Preparation 1
- *U.S. Air Force* *1*
- *Penn State University* *2*
- *IBM, East Fishkill, N.Y.* *3*
- *Summary Lessons Learned* *6*

CHAPTER 2   Launch 7
- *IBM Manassas, Virginia* *7*
- *Bromont, Canada* *9*
- *Department of Labor Contract* *9*
- *Advanced Systems Development Division* *10*
- *Personnel* *12*
- *Summary Lessons Learned* *13*

CHAPTER 3   Development 14
- *Safeguard* *15*
- *Postal Systems* *15*
- *Military Systems* *16*
- *Summary Lessons Learned* *18*

CHAPTER 4   Submarine Systems 19
- *Trainers* *20*
- *San Diego, California* *21*
- *Sub Base Bangor, Washington* *24*
- *Summary Lessons Learned* *26*

CHAPTER 5	FSD Headquarters	27
• Technical and Systems Planning		28
• Program Manager of Anti Submarine Warfare Systems		30
• Summary Lessons Learned		32
CHAPTER 6	Training and Development	34
• Interactive Television		34
• Learning Resource Centers		35
• IBM Personal Computer Training		35
• Customer Training		35
• Summary Lessons Learned		37
CHAPTER 7	Lobbyist	39
• Washington, D.C.		40
• Richmond, Virginia		40
• Summary Lessons Learned		43
CHAPTER 8	Technical Staff	44
• Technical Vitality		44
• Aspen Institute		46
• Harvard University		46
• Paris, France		47
• Moscow, U.S.S.R.		48
• NASA		52
Aerojet-General Corporation		53
McDonnell-Douglas Corporation		53
Software Engineering Institute (SEI)		53
• Software and Systems Resource Center (SSRC)		54
• Summary Lessons Learned		55
CHAPTER 9	Quarter Century Club	56
• Divestiture		56
• Acquisition		57
• Merger		57
• IBM Summary		58

- Summary Lessons Learned 59

Chapter 10 Loral 60
- Loral's SSRC 60
- Vought 62
- Librascope 62
- Goodyear Aerospace 62
- Loral, Salt Lake City 63
- Loral, Rancho San Margarita 63
- Summary Lessons Learned 64

Chapter 11 Lockheed Martin 65
- Boeing, Seattle, Washington 66
- Sunnyvale 66
- Fort Worth 67
- Orlando 67
- Denver 68
- New Orleans 68
- Indonesia 69
  - Jakarta 69
  - Bandung 70
  - Yogyakarta 72
- Valley Forge, Pa. 74
- Summary Lessons Learned 77

Chapter 12 Litton Industries/TASC 78
- The TASC Institute 79
- The Strategic Plan 79
- West Palm Beach, Florida 82
- Summary Lessons Learned 83

Chapter 13 Veridian 84
- The Veridian Institute 84
- The Pentagon, September 11, 2001 88
- The Last Year 90

- *Summary Lessons Learned* *91*

CHAPTER 14   Epilogue. 92

APPENDIX A   List of Some U.S. Locations Visited 95

APPENDIX B   List of Some Abbreviations. 97

About the Author 99

Index 101

Acknowledgments

I would like to acknowledge the support provided by my wife, Cheryl, who contributed her thoughts and suggestions that made this a better book. Her support was invaluable throughout my life and through the difficult times in my diverse careers. I would also like to acknowledge Zach, Chris, Matt, and Michele, our children, who all graduated from colleges and universities and are pursuing professional careers.

Preface

The purpose of this book is to chart the progress of my many careers in the defense industry over a period of thirty years. Looking back, it seems to have gone so quickly but the problems, travels, and adventures are as clear to me as if they happened yesterday. Defense industry professionals who are starting to think about their own career may be able to benefit from reading this narrative. When you're beginning a career, what you want to do can be a cause of concern and worry. Nevertheless, I've learned that your career finds you. You often don't find it unless you're one of the fortunate few who know what their life's pursuit will be and indeed wind up doing what you knew you would.

I never thought I'd be a defense contractor but after wandering through a wilderness of work force events, that's what others have called me. A defense contractor works for a private corporation that has contracts with the Federal Government. Department of Defense, (DOD), contracts often support the U.S. military and sometimes foreign governments. There are lots of careers one can pursue as a defense contractor. Engineers, software developers, business developers, purchasing agents, contract administrators, project managers, corporate trainers, and administrative support professionals are just a few of the many careers in this field. It's getting tougher to have continuity in a single career in the defense industry. Divestitures, acquisitions, and mergers have taken their toll on thousands of people.

I'm sure that some of the choices I made in the 1950's and 1960's helped shape my professional destiny. I know that if I had never graduated from high school, gone into the military, or graduated from college that my life would have turned out much differently. Later, it became clear to me that it wasn't only my choices that helped shape my career, it was also historic events, people that I met, and good fortune that helped me along.

Today, it is often said that young professionals will not have a career in the same sense as their parents. Many believe that young professionals will be working for many different companies during their life and that most will not be able to work for a single company until they retire. There is probably some truth to this line of thought. But professionals starting their career should not despair in this analysis. There is excitement and adventure that awaits young people in pursuit of their destiny. Some people may not want to work for the same company doing the same kind of job year after year. In my experience jobs always change and job security has always been a myth. Some might say my career with IBM that spanned 26 years was indicative of a time that is now long gone. I disagree. There are still possibilities of pursuing a career with an organization that would meet or exceed 26 years. Government and military service are some examples and in private enterprise, there are many others.

As you read the next chapters, you will note the high points and low points in my career as a defense contractor. You will follow multiple career paths that have taken me through corporate mergers, divestitures, and acquisitions. You'll travel with me on business trips with five different companies, to major cities around most of the United States, and to Europe, Canada, the former Soviet Union, Indonesia, and Asia. Although I spent a lot of my corporate years in training and development, you'll find that this wasn't one career played out in the theatre of business life. I had multiple careers in many companies and survived the ups and downs of corporate life on a road that eventually led me to witness the beginning of the war on terror at the Pentagon on September 11, 2001.

In the following chapters, I will describe the many different jobs and careers I've had starting with IBM. The divestiture of the IBM Federal Systems Company to Loral Corporation in 1994 changed my corporate identity and the way I viewed myself. Like many others I was caught up in a world of defense industry divestitures, mergers, and acquisitions. Lockheed Martin acquired Loral's Defense Systems business unit in 1996 and three years later, I was given a severance package from Lockheed Martin. I was entering my senior years when I was hired by TASC, Inc., a subsidiary of Litton Industries. Then, as the 20th century ended and TASC was acquired by Northrop Grumman I was hired by Veridian. Several years later, Veridian was acquired by General Dynamics.

I view my time in business as being able to successfully win, implement, and manage different defense contracts. It was my privilege to assist many employees of different corporations with their training and development goals. I was able to learn from and teach others about the rapidly changing technologies of the times. I was granted the unique opportunity with IBM to successfully lobby important issues with elected officials. Through two corporations I was able to successfully conduct international business. In the final years of my career, I developed two web based corporate institutes for two different defense corporations.

It is my sincere hope that you can benefit from these memoirs and lessons learned, that your career is as rewarding and exciting as mine was, and that you're a success in whatever industry or professional career you've chosen.

T.H. Henning
Haymarket, Virginia
July 14, 2005

1

Preparation

When I graduated from Shaler High School in Glenshaw, Pa. in June, 1959, I had no idea where I was going or what I was going to do with my life. The Soviet Union had launched the first earth satellite, Sputnik, in October, 1957 and my last two years of high school emphasized math and science. Many young men and women in my high school class were headed for college to study engineering and science, and others were headed to vocational schools. I was searching for a job with the rest of my high school class. My grades and economic situation ruled out any options to continue on to college or attend a vocational school. The only options for me appeared to be to continue to work at the Atlantic White Tower, Inc. restaurants in Pittsburgh, Pa., where I had worked summers and evenings for the past three years while in high school, find a better job, or to join the U.S. military. I had applied for entry to the U.S. Air Force Academy and was interviewed by a selection panel, but I wasn't accepted. I had also applied for the Air Cadet Program to train to become a pilot in the Air Force, but poor test results disqualified me from pursuing that option. Finally, I went to the U.S. Post Office on the North Side of Pittsburgh and enlisted in the U.S. Air Force. On September 18, 1959, I took the oath to defend my country and was sworn into military service.

U.S. AIR FORCE

After completing Basic Military Training at Lackland Air Force Base in San Antonio, Texas in December, 1959, I received a top secret security clearance and went to an intelligence school at Goodfellow Air Force Base in San Angelo, Texas, from January, 1960 to August, 1960. That summer, a sandstorm had struck the area and as I held on to a rope and groped my way in pitch darkness from building to building on the base through the sandstorm, I promised myself that I would further my education and eventually get a college degree. After graduation from the Air Force technical school, I was sent to serve out my next three years overseas at Royal Air Force Station, Kirknewton, Scotland in the Pentland Hills outside of Edinburgh, Scotland. Not everyone was selected for duty in Europe. Some of us went to Southeast Asia, the Middle East, and other corners of the world. I didn't know it at the time, but I had taken the first steps to prepare myself for a career as a defense contractor; first high school graduation, and second, joining the military. Having a military background is not essential for a career as a defense contractor, but it helps since the U.S. military is one of the main customers of defense corporations. I traveled extensively while I was in Europe. I went to England, Germany, France, Holland, Belgium, Denmark, and Sweden. I even attended a short course at Cambridge University, and successfully completed one year of Russian language and other college courses at the University of Maryland's continuing education center in Scotland.

PENN STATE UNIVERSITY

After completing military service, I transferred my college credits to The Pennsylvania State University, at University Park, Pa., and started my sophomore year at the main campus in 1963. I started the first semester majoring in civil engineering, but since my first semester grades were low enough to almost get me ousted from college, I quickly transferred into the College of Liberal Arts and changed my major to political science and Russian area studies. I still had no idea where I was going, but my grades improved so much that I was placed on the deans list during my junior and senior years. I was able to graduate with a Bachelor of Arts degree in 1966 and fulfill the promise I made to myself in the sandstorm at San Angelo, Texas. I also received a certificate in Russian area studies. I was the first in my family history to ever graduate from college. While walking on the Penn State campus one evening I had a premonition that one day I would visit the Soviet Union. It was a weird sensation and seemed very far out, surreal, and unrealistic. I thought that I'd never get to visit the Soviet Union.

After graduation I went to the college placement center and scheduled interviews with commercial banks, the Central Intelligence Agency, and corporations like Westinghouse and IBM. I thought about getting a job with the Federal Government and traveled by bus to Washington, D.C. where I was interviewed by the U.S. Office of Education. Since I didn't get any good job offers, I returned to Penn State and applied to the Graduate School of Education where I was accepted as a candidate for a Masters degree in higher education. The Vietnam

War was tearing the country apart in 1966 and I helped returning Vietnam veterans adjust to academic life at Penn State. The university had offered me a permanent position as a residence hall area coordinator and the job helped me pay for the next two years of college. College graduates were trying to get into graduate school to avoid the draft and openings were scarce so I felt fortunate that I was admitted to the Graduate School of Education. My career thinking shifted to possibly getting a job as a college administrator or teacher. Two years later, I graduated with a Masters degree in Higher Education. Then, out of the blue, IBM sent me a letter telling me they were visiting the campus and that they'd like to talk to me about a job. They had retained my application from two years earlier. I was so impressed that I jumped at the chance to talk to the recruiter who came to campus that spring.

IBM had a job opening for an instructor in their Skills Training Department at the East Fishkill, New York, Components Division, (CD) facility. It was amazing to me, that IBM, the best computer company in the world at the time, staffed with talented engineers and scientists, would be interested in hiring me, who failed computer science in college and who had not majored in business. Yet, I was hired and started work at IBM on July 8, 1968. Sometimes good fortune plays a part in your career when you least expect it.

IBM, EAST FISHKILL, N.Y.

I relocated from State College, Pa. to East Fishkill, N.Y. and started my career with IBM. At the time, I thought my career was to be in the education department of the corporation at the East Fishkill, New York location. I envisioned working there the rest of my life. But, while this was an important start, my career would take many more twists and turns in the future.

Everything at IBM impressed me. I started taking evening courses in engineering education subjects. I took technical tours of the product lines and learned a great deal about how semiconductors were manufactured. Later I was asked to conduct technical tours for customers and foreign visitors. Most of all, I worked very hard to show IBM that they'd hired the right person. I taught basic courses in economic ordering quantity analysis, effective business presentations, and new employee orientation. I helped introduce computer assisted testing for technicians and manufacturing operators, coordinated skills training sessions, evaluated secretarial training, made suggestions for improvements, and monitored management development sessions at the Kenyon House, a former rubber baron's mansion, in Poughkeepsie, N.Y. I visited local colleges and traveled to the components division plant at Burlington, Vermont. I attended instructor training at the Princeton Club in New York City where I was videotaped and critiqued to improve my teaching style. In the summer of 1968, I was selected to attend a conference of future IBM Personnel Department leaders at Kerhonksen, N.Y. in the Catskill Mountains. That fall, I was selected to go deep sea fishing with top IBM corporate executives and attend a leadership conference in Atlantic City, New Jersey. I felt honored and accepted in the corporation. I was on my way to becoming an IBM leader, and maybe a manager, someday.

I learned about the scope of training and education programs at IBM which at the time were:

- New Employee Orientation—All new employees attended NEO and learned about the company and its history.
- Manufacturing Skills Training—There were hundreds of machine operators who had to learn about substrate manufacturing processes and equipment.
- Administrative job training for non-technical workers—Secretaries, staff support groups like purchasing, finance, and personnel all had training programs tailored to their needs.
- Engineering Education—All engineers attended courses designed for their engineering specialties.
- Voluntary Education—An off company time program was provided for continuing education open to all employees and covering many topics.
- Technician Training—There were hundreds of technicians who had to learn about the so called "device" manufacturing processes and equipment which included advanced courses in how to make transistors the size of a period at the end of this sentence. Additionally, there were technicians that serviced IBM products that had their own training facility.
- Marketing and Sales training—IBM was known for its marketing and sales training schools and all marketing and sales representatives attended months of training before being assigned to branch offices.
- Tuition reimbursement programs—IBM reimbursed any employee who sought to pursue higher education, and

- Management Development—All managers, no matter what level they had attained in the corporation, went to IBM local management schools at the division level, and on to the IBM Management Development Center in Armonk, N.Y. for advanced training.

I liked the Mid Hudson Valley, the short trips to IBM Headquarters in Armonk, N.Y., and commuting by train from Beacon-Newburgh to Grand Central Station in New York City. I liked staying at the Barbizon Plaza Hotel, going to the Playboy Club, attending theatres on Broadway, and going out to dinner at Jack Dempsey's restaurant in Times Square. I was preparing to launch my career, but I was to find out later that ***a career is a lot like a jigsaw puzzle—you don't see the full picture until the puzzle has been put together.***

In 1969, IBM announced it was starting up a new components division facility at Manassas, Virginia. The general manager and other top executives who were selected to start up the new facility came to East Fishkill and presented their plans for the new site. I was given an opportunity for promotion into the training department that was forming at the new site if I would transfer to Manassas. It was a great opportunity and although I had been at East Fishkill for less than a year, I accepted the job offer. I was one of the first 25 people to start up what would become a huge, multi-division facility in a few years.

Different people played an important role in my career. Those that saw merit in my job performance recommended me for transfers, raises, and promotions. Those that didn't think I was as competitive as others for promotional opportunities tried to slow down my career. There were a lot of talented people at IBM that management could choose for upward movement in the corporation and competition for each job was tough.

Although I didn't foresee it at the time, the Skills Training Department reported to the Personnel function and Personnel did not see a career for me in training and development. They wanted me to transfer to other personnel departments such as recruiting, placement, benefits, and compensation. Senior personnel management at East Fishkill thought that a transfer to IBM's newest facility in Manassas, Virginia would accelerate my interest in a career in Personnel and endorsed my promotion and transfer. I had no interest in other personnel departments and felt more comfortable identifying with the training mission. This would change as my career was launched at the new CD plant and lab in Manassas, Virginia.

SUMMARY LESSONS LEARNED

- Prepare for a life long journey by getting as much formal education as you can.

- Learn as much as you can about the organization that offers you a job before you accept the offer.

- Don't rely on good fortune, but when it comes your way be sure to capitalize on it.

- Take every opportunity to accept every promotion that comes your way <u>except</u> if it causes disruption in your family or personal life.

- Work hard and continue learning throughout your life.

- Be professional, courteous, and kind to everyone.

2

Launch

Manassas, Virginia is perhaps best known for the "Battle of Bull Run" which occurred in July, 1861, at the outbreak of the American Civil War. Manassas was a beautiful small town in the spring of 1969. Magnolia trees and flowers blossomed, a small two lane road led from the newly built route 66 to the main town center, and new town homes were under construction around the area. The Battlefield Park was on the outskirts of the town and attracted tourists every year.

IBM MANASSAS, VIRGINIA

IBM paid all of my relocation costs and covered my expenses until I found an apartment. The company had leased office space in a small shopping center while a temporary prefabricated building was under construction at the main site. I was given a small office at the shopping center and quickly got to know all of the top executives and newly hired personnel in the office. I was promoted to the position of Senior Associate Instructor in the IBM Manassas Training Department which was given the responsibility for all employee training and management development programs. My first priority was to coordinate and conduct the technical training for new hires and transfers from the components division plants in East Fishkill and Burlington. Many IBM employees did not want to transfer to Manassas and as a result, the new facility had to hire many local people who did not have an understanding of the IBM Corporation, its technologies, or the components business. There were no classroom facilities so we leased space at the Sinclair Elementary School in Manassas, and taught classes in new employee orientation, substrate manufacturing processes, and technician training. During the evening voluntary education classes in finance, interpersonal communications, and other topics were conducted. The new plant start-up operations presented another learning experience and we were often confronted with new problems to solve outside of the area of training and development. We were involved in facilities planning issues, community impact issues, traffic lights, railroad crossing signs, geologic issues, local housing issues, and coordination with officials from the town of Manassas and County of Prince William. By September of 1969, we had started producing components and shipping them back to the major plants in New York and Vermont. The components were small, dime sized squares called Solid Logic Technology, (SLT). These so called "chips" contained circuits and very small sized transistors. They were then inserted onto boards and became part of the electronic package that formed the heart of the IBM 360 computer series. IBM made a lot of money on the IBM 360 and established itself as the leading computer company in the world. By the end of the year, we had moved into prefabricated buildings on the site. IBM Manassas had a population of 500 people and celebrated its first year by inviting the community to tour the facility and share in a huge birthday cake.

I was given the responsibility to conduct the first management training session for IBM at Manassas. With the help of senior management, we developed a one week training program for new managers. The session was held at the Airlie House near Warrenton, Virginia. I taught a session on Program Evaluation and Review Techniques, (PERT), and arranged the course agenda, schedule, workbooks, and coordination of the class. It was evaluated as being very successful. A few months later, I was promoted to my first management position in IBM, Manager of Training and Development. I didn't know it at the time, but it would be my last promotion for the next eight years. My manager had more than 40 years experience in IBM and filled me in on the history of the corporation. I learned from him that *senior people have a very different view of time than young people*. To him, eight years was a very short period of time, but to me, it was an eternity. At the time, the first level of management was the highest one could achieve in training and development. If I wanted to go further in my career I would have to leave the training department and transfer into another Personnel department. In just under two years, I had been promoted several times and into a management position in IBM. I was considered to be on the fast track, but my experience in the corporation was primarily in the training area so there were plans to move me into other Personnel departments as soon as possible. It was then that we received notice that another components division plant was starting up in Bromont, Canada, just outside Montreal. There was heavy unemployment in French Canada at the time and Manassas was given the responsibility to help with the new plant start-up since we had been successful with the new start-up in

Virginia. We also had the mission to train the Canadian employees that would be hired from the French Canadian province.

BROMONT, CANADA

This was my first exposure to IBM outside the United States and I traveled to Montreal and Bromont frequently during the cold winter of 1970-1971. Since French Canadian was the spoken language, we hired a French speaking Canadian to help us with teaching and translating components division technical terms. That year we trained hundreds of new Canadian employees and got the plant up and running in record time. I still remember those below zero winter temperatures and the warmth of the French Canadian people. As a reward for the training start up, I received an engraved silver bowl from IBM along with a reward check.

During my second year as a manager, I began teaching a course called "Introduction to Business" at the Northern Virginia Community College which was leasing space in the local high school. The college president was planning to move into a new building at the college campus located near the Manassas Battlefield Park and was pleased with the support provided by IBM. I liked the training and development field and my career had progressed well in the first few years. I was anxious about what my next career move would be and was hopeful that I could stay longer in my current job. To help prolong my stay in the position, I was supportive of a recruiting goal to hire the so called "hard core" unemployed people from the area and proposed that we could train and develop those people we hired to make them fully productive assembly line operators in a few months.

DEPARTMENT OF LABOR CONTRACT

Under a contract with the U.S. Department of Labor and in cooperation with the National Alliance of Businessmen, (NAB), we hired a group of 20 people. The Department of Labor and NAB certified that they were, by their definition, "hard core" unemployed. I personally never liked the term "hard core" because it sounded like the word "incorrigible", and I found most of the new hires to be shy, nervous, and eager to succeed. Most of them did not possess a high school diploma. Many had trouble reading and comprehending instructions. For most of them this was their first full time job and they had to be taught how to read and understand their paycheck statement. Some had family and health problems. The program was planned and implemented as follows:

- First step was to structure a program that had a mixture of job training, preparation for the high school GED exam, and tutoring for those that needed counseling and personal assistance. A computer assisted instruction, (CAI), lab was set up which provided courses in remedial math and English. The lab was very successful in raising the skill levels of many in the class. The traditional classroom was rearranged, painted, and seating was modified into a circular arrangement.
- Second step was to hire an instructor who had the personal attributes, knowledge, and skills to be able to handle a variety of problems that would occur in and out of the classroom. The instructor would also work closely with the employee's managers during the course of instruction.
- Third step was for IBM to provide back up medical and legal assistance if needed.
- Finally, we implemented the daytime work-study training program.

Six months later, only one of the original twenty employees had dropped out of the program and left the business. The remaining employees passed the GED exam and received their high school general education diplomas. They had lunch with the plant general manager upon their graduation from the program. Most of them were succeeding in their jobs and one of the original twenty went on to take courses at the local community college. The Department of Labor and the NAB was pleased with the results and the program was highlighted in the local newspaper. With the help of the course instructor, I had successfully completed my first government contract.

ADVANCED SYSTEMS DEVELOPMENT DIVISION

It was about this time, in 1972, that the Advanced Systems Development Division, (ASDD), relocated to Manassas from Poughkeepsie, N.Y. This was a separate product development division which had a different mission than the components division. One of their senior engineers came into my office to visit one afternoon. He had one flipchart which he taped to the wall. On it was an illustration of a terminal and new product that he wanted to develop that had applications for education and training as well as other fields. This instructional delivery system was a standalone terminal that could be programmed to store audio and visual information. He asked me to join him as a staff systems engineer to assist in developing the new product. Flattered by the "systems engineering" title, and not wanting to move into other Personnel departments, I saw an opportunity to get in on the ground floor of something that might turn into an IBM product line. I jumped at the chance and accepted a lateral move as a staff systems engineer into ASDD. Since I didn't know what a systems engineer was, I imagined what it would be like to be an IBM systems engineer. I thought it remarkable that a liberal arts and education graduate like me could have a career as a systems engineer in a high technology corporation like IBM. The Personnel manager was disappointed to see me move out of the components division and into another career field altogether. He said that I might regret the move and it turned out he was right.

The next year was like starting all over again in IBM. I had to learn new terminology, new product development processes, quality terms, and technical tasks. I learned how to program what at that time was called an E-prom device which contained instruction sets for the delivery system. I enrolled in a doctoral program at The American University to study the emerging field of educational technology. I traveled to the IBM labs at Los Gatos, California and the Thomas J. Watson Research Center at Yorktown Heights, New York. I actually worked for a time at the Yorktown Heights lab with an IBM 1130 computer and Sylvania light table to create some of the first computer generated animations. I traveled to the Science Research Associates lab in Chicago, Illinois and obtained individualized program instruction materials that were used in public schools at the time. They would become part of the new instructional system demo. I programmed the system and tested the system. I learned about diagnostics and listened and learned from the real systems engineers who were also developing the system. I became a charter member of the Society for Applied Learning Technology and went to Miami, Florida to attend their conferences. I traveled to San Francisco and the IBM San Jose plant site. As I was tasked to develop the software and courseware for the system, I traveled to the IBM plant in Rochester, Minnesota to learn about film and media at their advanced media center. During this time, I started to become an educational technologist and began to gain confidence in this new career identity. Without an engineering degree, I knew I couldn't go far in ASDD but the combination of working on a new product, learning the systems engineering vocabulary, and studying for my doctorate at The American University opened up new horizons for me. Then the bubble burst! A senior executive from corporate headquarters reviewed the proposed new product which resulted in its cancellation. As I recall, the major problem was that the technology wasn't seen as long term, the costs exceeded the targets, and the corporate executive just didn't believe that this was a product that IBM was willing to invest in. It turned out in retrospect that his decision was the right one. Everything was boxed up and the product sent to an IBM warehouse in upstate New York which I understood was the graveyard of wannabe IBM products that never made it. And my systems engineering career hopes vanished along with the end of that project.

Personnel

In 1973, there was nowhere for me to go except back to the Personnel manager in the components division and ask him if he still had a place for me in one of his Personnel departments. As it turned out, he placed me in the recruiting and placement department and a few months later moved the manager of that department into a second level management position. I was named Manager of Recruiting and Placement. While I was thankful to be employed, I didn't like the job. Thousands of applicants competed for hundreds of positions. The job involved visits to college campuses, processing applications and other paperwork, making decisions about moving and living expenses, going to recruitment fairs, filling employee requirement openings, and managing the other recruiters in the department. After several months in the job, I asked to be moved to another department and joined Employee Relations. From the Personnel manager's perspective, this was another career limiting move. The employee relations job involved handling employee grievances, counseling managers who were not doing the kind of job IBM expected, and conducting the annual IBM opinion survey. I enjoyed being a personnel researcher for a time and working with an IBM industrial psychologist in developing and analyzing opinion surveys. We traveled to the IBM Poughkeepsie plant to use the IBM 370 computer to process the survey data from two divisions. We both received awards for conducting the survey but, I knew that without a PhD in industrial psychology, I wouldn't have a career as a personnel researcher.

Then, fortune intervened once again. The Federal Systems Division, (FSD), in Gaithersburg, Maryland had job openings. The Systems Training Department there had heard of my work in ASDD and had an opportunity for an instructional systems developer and instructor. FSD was IBM's division that managed all Federal Government contracts and I had a chance to enter a new occupation in a new division and learn about government contracting.

Although it was a lateral move, I accepted the job in FSD in 1973 and started down the path of becoming a defense contractor. I had only been in IBM five years but had changed divisions 3 times, (CD, ASDD, and FSD). I had changed jobs multiple times, (Training instructor, Training Manager, Systems Engineering Product Developer, Personnel Manager of Recruiting and Placement, Employee Relations Representative, and Personnel Researcher). Each job could have led me to a different career path.

In IBM, having a sponsor in a senior management position in an established functional area was important to ones progress. I had lost sponsorship from the Personnel function. I hadn't been in the systems engineering function long enough to gain sponsorship there, and I had reached the top of the training and development career path after I had been made manager of that department. I had not stayed in management or any job long enough to gain sponsorship. After five years, I was moving laterally and going nowhere.

SUMMARY LESSONS LEARNED

- **Changing jobs too often causes you to lose career sponsorship.**
- **Exploring new jobs can be interesting but doesn't necessarily lead to promotional opportunities.**
- **If you choose to take lateral assignments, be sure that you will be able to acquire knowledge, skills, or attributes that will serve you well in the future.**
- **Learn from senior leaders. They've been down the path you're walking and often have excellent advice.**
- **Understand that senior people think of time differently than younger people.**

3

Development

In 1973, I sold my townhouse in Manassas and moved to Gaithersburg, Maryland. The IBM Federal Systems Division, (FSD), facility in Gaithersburg was considerably larger than the Manassas site at the time. Federal Systems Headquarters was located in Bethesda, Maryland, not far from the Gaithersburg site. It may be hard for many people to think of IBM as a defense contractor, but FSD was a division of about 10,000 people who were committed to providing products and services to the Federal Government and supporting the national interest. IBM had supported the military as far back as World War II and was proud of their support to the government and the achievements of FSD. Besides Gaithersburg, there were FSD locations in Houston, Texas, Owego, New York, Westlake, California, and later Rockville, Maryland and Manassas, Virginia. FSD in Manassas would soon be supporting the U.S. Navy submarine service.

There were several large government contracts that sustained the Gaithersburg facility. Among them, contracts with NASA, the Safeguard contract with the Department of Defense, the Command and Control Systems Engineering and Integration, (CCS SE&I), contract with the U.S. Navy, and the Advanced Optical Character Reader, (AOCR) contract with the U.S. Post Office. Several people in my department worked in the Pentagon and FSD technical representatives could be found almost anywhere working on classified projects at customer premises. I started teaching again at Montgomery College in Germantown, Maryland in the evenings. Prior to moving to their main campus, courses were taught at a nearby high school. They promoted me from adjunct instructor to adjunct professor of business and I taught several business and management courses there part time in the evening for the next eight years.

SAFEGUARD

I was granted a Department of Defense Top Secret Clearance and put to work on the Safeguard Project making videotaped training sessions for the U.S. military. Safeguard was an anti-missile missile that was supposed to be deployed around military targets in the U.S. The technology was in the early stages and the contract didn't last long, so I was reassigned to work on the Advanced Optical Character Reader for the U.S. Post Office.

POSTAL SYSTEMS

The Advanced Optical Character Reader, (AOCR), consisted of an IBM 370 computer and special hardware and software that would optically recognize the characters on machine printed mail and then sort the mail into the proper bins for pickup and delivery. I was tasked with developing an AOCR Supervisors Handbook and then using the handbook as a textbook, train the supervisors on the new system. I worked closely with engineers and programmers to develop the handbook and learned how to develop it in a technical manual format. I wondered if I could pursue a career as a technical writer. I guess I did a good job on the AOCR Handbook because I was assigned to write more technical manuals on contracts that I would work on in the future. In parallel, I developed a series of flipcharts and transparencies. They were the primary classroom aids at the time. I traveled by train to visit the New York City main post office where the AOCR was to be installed. The main post office was near Penn Central Station. I toured the facility and met the supervisors who I would be training.

When the system was installed and tested and the handbook and course materials were ready, I traveled again to the central post office in New York City and discovered that the training was scheduled between midnight and daybreak. During the day, I slept at the Hilton Hotel near Penn Central Station and at night I walked several blocks to the main post office to conduct the training session. As I recall, the training session was about a week long and afterwards, I returned to Gaithersburg, happy to be back on the day shift.

MILITARY SYSTEMS

After a short trip to Lexington, Kentucky to help with the training of office equipment systems engineers, I was assigned to developing technical courses for the U.S. Army and U.S. Navy. All course materials for the training of military personnel were developed in accordance with military specifications and I learned about data item descriptions, (DIDs), contract line items, (CLINS), and military specifications such as OD 45519.

It was important to read the contract provisions, usually the L and M sections of the contract, which described the system and the systems training requirements. In the case of the U.S. Navy, there were Personnel Performance Profiles, (PPPs), Training Level Assignments, (TLAs), Objective Assignment Charts, (OACs), and a strict instructional systems design process that had to be followed.

In support of U.S. Army contracts, I traveled to Fort Monmouth, New Jersey to learn how the U.S. Army trained personnel in basic electricity and electronics. Computer assisted instruction also was used there at the time. I also traveled to Fortress Monroe in Virginia, home of the U.S. Army's Training and Doctrine Command, (TRADOC). There, I taught a communications course for Army helicopter pilots and was invited to nearby Hampton Institute as a guest speaker in the graduate school of business. Years later, I briefed a U.S. Army major general from TRADOC and contributed to the U.S. Army's Vision for the year 2010.

After the U.S. Army contracts, I was tasked to support the CCS SE&I team at Gaithersburg. I helped design a trainer and curriculum for a small subsystem of the Trident Submarine called the Monitoring Subsystem. This subsystem would monitor the noise made by the submarine.

In 1974, IBM in Owego decided to transfer the largest contract that FSD had ever won to Manassas. The AN/BQQ-5 Sonar System that would be installed on U.S. Navy Fleet "fast attack" nuclear submarines would be developed in Manassas. The sonar system was designed for installation on the new SSN, (Submersible Ship Nuclear), Los Angeles Class submarines but was also modified to be backfitted on existing submarines. The AN/BQQ-6 Sonar System that would be installed on the U.S. Navy's SSBN, (Submersible Ship Ballistic Nuclear) Ohio Submarine, the first of a new class of Trident nuclear missile submarines, would also be developed in Manassas. A submarine sonar operator trainer called the 21B64 would be developed by IBM for the fast attack submarine training and a Trident Sonar Operator Trainer, (TSOT), would be developed to train the Trident submarine crews. We began work on the curriculum that would train U.S. Navy submarine sonar technicians, officers, and shipyard personnel in the operations and maintenance of both sonar systems and both trainers. In Gaithersburg, the CCS SE&I mission was also transferred to Manassas.

In 1975 I sold the house I bought in Gaithersburg and rented a townhouse in Centreville, Virginia, not far from Manassas. A new Integrated Logistics Support, (ILS), engineering function was being formed and the Gaithersburg Systems Training Department that I was part of became part of that organization. ILS was the organization that provided field maintenance support, spare parts, technical manuals, life cycle product engineering support, product testing, and training along with other military product support functions. It was a technical organization that worked closely with systems engineering and generated profit for the division. Many ILS engineers were members of the Society for Logistics Engineering and the organization was staffed with former Navy submarine officers and logistics engineers.

The Manassas facility had grown to almost 3,000 people by this time and with the sonar systems mission being transferred from Owego, New York, the population of the site grew even more over the next few years. Additionally, the components division mission had grown and monolithic systems technology had replaced the older solid logic technology. The technology to develop transistors that were placed on the manufactured substrates was also transferred from East Fishkill and new clean rooms and high technology labs involving processes like silicon crystal growth, wafer dicing, photo etching and photo resist now became part of the expanded components division mission. The Advanced Systems Development Division, (ASDD), presence in Manassas was also expanding to address small systems input and output product development. With FSD expanding its presence on the site, many functions had to be relocated throughout the town of Manassas in leased space until more buildings could be constructed on the main site to house the expanding missions. ILS would be located in the Virginia Bank Building on Sudley Road.

SUMMARY LESSONS LEARNED

- Learning how the government does business might take many years.

- Relocating to another state or geographic location more than 50 miles from your current workplace can be an expensive proposition. Be sensitive to family concerns and if they aren't supportive of your move, see if you can negotiate a different deal.

- Being a defense contractor can be hazardous work, can involve foreign travel, and exposure to dangerous conditions. Is this a career for you?

- Defense contractors need to learn about finance, accounting, contracts, procurement, business development, software development, systems engineering, product development, systems integration, and program management.

4

Submarine Systems

Everything seemed to fall apart over the next few years. My first marriage failed, I dropped out of the doctorate program at American University, my health failed, and my career was in shambles. One of the IBM senior managers scheduled a meeting with me because of a drop in my performance. He said that I wasn't a hardware, software, or systems engineer and it was hard for him to find a place for me in the Integrated Logistics Support Engineering organization. He suggested that I improve my performance, said he would give me a chance to succeed, and encouraged me to start learning the skills I would need to survive in the new organization. I left the interview depressed, worried, and unsure of myself. **The IBM that I had joined seven years ago seemed far away. It had been replaced by a colder, more technical, and more competitive business environment. Or maybe it had always been that way and the" honeymoon" often given young new employees was over.** I now had to put into practice the lessons learned from developmental assignments that I had been given and earn money for the corporation.

In the beginning, I didn't know anything about submarines. I started to read books on the submarine service. I learned that "fast attack" nuclear submarines were designated SSN's and their mission was to find and attack enemy ships, submarines, and other vessels as well as conduct undersea surveillance and support intelligence missions. I learned that nuclear "ballistic missile" submarines were designated as SSBN's and since they carried strategic nuclear ballistic weapons, their mission was to go to sea and "hide" from the enemy so they could launch their missiles in the event of nuclear war. These "boomers" as they were called had two crews, a "gold" crew and a "blue" crew that rotated sea duty. I read about the history of the "silent service" and went aboard old World War II diesel submarines which now were floating museums. I studied the different component departments of a submarine and learned how they worked together. I toured mock ups of submarines being built. I learned about anti submarine warfare and took courses in acoustics and the properties of sound in the ocean from IBM and U.S. Navy instructors. Little by little, I learned a great deal about submarines.

I went to work on proposals for a new Sonar Operator Trainer, called the 21B64. When the contract was won, I was tasked with developing a technical operating manual for the system and leading a team to develop a seven week operations and maintenance course for U.S. Navy submarine instructors. I spent all of 1975 and 1976 working with systems engineers, systems integrators, and programmers in the IBM labs in Manassas where the trainer and sonar systems were being developed. In accordance with U.S. Navy specifications, I developed the personnel performance profiles, training level assignments, objective assignment charts, course outlines, curriculum, and instructional support materials for the AN/BQQ-5 sonar system and the 21B64 Sonar Operator Trainer. All curriculum materials had to be cross referenced to the technical manuals.

TRAINERS

The pre-production Sonar Operator Trainer, 21B64, was the first trainer that IBM ever built. The 21B64 was comprised of three control display consoles that were the same as those that would be installed on fast attack submarines. In addition, it had an instructor console, a Univac computer, and many other hardware units that would typically be located in the sonar area of the submarine. The trainer would simulate a submarine in the ocean and submarine sonar operators would sit at the consoles and perform the tactical operations with the trainer that they would later perform at sea. I had to learn the operations and maintenance for the entire system well enough to write a technical manual for the system, well enough to develop the seven week course for the system, and well enough to teach the two week operations portion of the course to experienced submarine instructors. The five week maintenance portion of the course would be taught by another IBM instructor who was a former IBM field engineer.

This was a technical challenge that snapped me out of my depression. As distinguished from trainers, IBM also built simulators that simulated equipment faults and system failures. But simulators did not provide for the operational scenarios that would confront sonar operator trainees using the 21B64. Simulators were comprised of tactical hardware and diagnostic software that were used by instructors to teach unit and system maintenance skills. Trainers required the development of classified operational scenarios and I had to learn sonar operations from former submariners.

Much of the 21B64 Trainer course would be classified. I spent many nights, weekends, and most of my working time in IBM labs working with engineers who were engaged in developing and integrating the system. This was the birth of new discipline-systems integration. IBM had been on the forefront of developing new technical careers. IBM was doing computer science before there was a career called computer science. IBM employees were programming computers before there was a programming profession. IBM was doing software development and systems engineering before they became popular occupations and fields of study. And IBM was doing systems integration before it became a field unto itself. Systems integration involved integrating hardware units made by IBM with units made by other equipment manufacturers and integrating software developed by IBM with software programs made by other equipment manufacturers. Not only did I have to learn the IBM hardware and software, but also the hardware and software developed by other manufacturers. I surprised myself in learning how to operate the maintenance and operations panel on the AN/UYK-7 computer and later became quite proficient with all the equipment used in the system and its operational capabilities. I first used the 21B64 in factory training sessions to train Navy sonar technicians and officers. I worked alongside former U.S. Navy submarine officers and sonar technicians and learned the jargon and communications processes used by submariners at sea. I learned how to run diagnostic tests and repair system faults and failures so that I could support my team partner, the other 21B64 IBM instructor. After awhile I became very proficient operating the control display console, and in using the AN/BQQ-5 sonar system and its 21B64 trainer. In 1977, I was selected to be the lead instructor for the 21B64 which would be installed in San Diego, California. This was a key assignment since success would mean that the Navy would purchase more trainers and failure would mean the end of my career.

SAN DIEGO, CALIFORNIA

I had never been in San Diego before the summer of 1977 and when I traveled there on business I instantly fell in love with the city. I stayed in an inn on Shelter Island that looked out over San Diego Bay. I was fascinated by the ships, fishing boats, submarines, and sailboats in the busy harbor. One boat, the "Egabrag" was San Diego Bay's garbage boat and its name was derived by spelling garbage backwards. I bought paintings of ships and lighthouses by local artists, went sailing on San Diego Bay, and toured the San Diego area.

As the lead instructor for the 21B64 Sonar Operator Trainer, I would support the installation of the trainer at the Fleet Anti Submarine Warfare Training Center, Pacific, and make sure that all materials for the operations and maintenance course had arrived. I met with the Training Center Commander and was introduced to the sonar chiefs and submarine sonar instructors who would participate in the course. These people were the best of the best in the submarine service and after I trained them, they would train the future submarine sonar sailors to use this new sonar system. The 21B64 would be their primary training aid for sonar operations training. Aside from factory tours and familiarization sessions, this would also be their first introduction to the new AN/BQQ-5 Sonar System. I was there to answer their questions and to teach them as well as learn from them.

The course was a high profile event that attracted submarine captains, officers, admirals, and even the Secretary of the Navy who stopped by during the training session to see the 21B64 and how Los Angeles Class submariners would be trained in the future. As the course proceeded, I earned the respect of the students which was important to me. When the admirals and the Secretary of the Navy stopped in to see a session in progress, they saw U.S. Navy instructors sitting at the control display consoles and manning the trainer instructor console. As the students were involved in the simulation of a submarine sailing beneath the ocean, the room was darkened and with all of the multi colored display lights blinking, it looked very impressive to the distinguished visitors. When senior IBM executives in Manassas learned that high ranking admirals and the Secretary of the Navy had visited the course, they asked me to call them and give them a status report of the visit. I think they were surprised at the high level of attention and wished that they had been in San Diego to meet and greet the Navy leaders. At any rate, the word of the success of the operations and maintenance course got back to the main plant before we did. The sonar instructors were very pleased and offered us a harbor cruise on a fast attack submarine. We traveled to Point Loma in San Diego and boarded the SSN 672 Pintado. It had been commissioned in September of 1971. We toured the boat, talked to the crew, ate in the galley, climbed up the sail, walked through the torpedo area, and at the end of our cruise, got a picture of the submarine. I later got a submarine SSN 572 Pintado patch. The submariners referred to us as "tech reps" from IBM. At the end of the course we left San Diego and returned to Manassas. Soon after, to the delight of all of us at IBM, the U.S. Navy ordered several more 21B64 trainers and several more Trident Sonar Operator Trainers. When the contract ended eighteen years later in 1995, 100 AN/BQQ-5 sonar systems were delivered to Navy Submarine fleet SSN's and 25 AN/BQQ-6 sonar systems were delivered to the Trident Submarine fleet SSBN's.

The Trident Sonar Operator Trainer, (TSOT), and the AN/BQQ-6 sonar system were the next challenge. I was named one of the lead instructors for sonar operator training for the SSBN Ohio Trident Submarine. It was my privilege to provide the sonar officers from the Ohio with factory training using the TSOT. In July, 1978, I was promoted to the position of Manager of Submarine Sonar Systems Training in ILS. After eight long years, I was back in management. When I remarried in October of that same year, and our youngest son was born a year later, everything seemed right again.

As the Manager of Submarine Sonar Systems Training, I was now responsible for all AN/BQQ-5 and AN/BQQ-6 sonar training. In addition, I assumed responsibility for developing new and follow on business. A team of instructors in Newport, Rhode Island reported to me, a team of instructors at San Diego reported to me, and a team of instructors at Sub Base Bangor, Washington reported to me. I traveled frequently to all of those locations throughout 1978 and 1979 and, acting as a representative of the IBM Submarine Systems Program Office, won new and follow on business with the customer.

The SSBN 726 Ohio Submarine was going on sea trials in June of 1981 so all of the sonar and crew training had to precede the sea trials. The TSOT operations and maintenance course was conducted by my team at Sub Base Bangor in October, 1979.

That fall, I was asked to give a presentation at the Naval War College in New London, Connecticut, and describe the 26 week training program to high ranking naval officers. The presentation was so well received that afterwards one officer asked me when I had attended the U.S. Naval Academy. When I told him that I was a veteran of the U.S. Air Force he found it hard to believe and complimented me on the presentation which he thought was outstanding. I told him that I was reflecting the work of many dedicated IBM professionals and former

U.S. Navy submariners who taught me well. While in New London, I visited Groton, Connecticut to meet with U.S. Navy shipyard personnel where the Ohio Submarine was being built, and then went on to Newport, Rhode Island to meet with Naval Undersea Systems Center, (NUSC) engineers.

SUB BASE BANGOR, WASHINGTON

In May of 1980, I traveled to Bangor, Washington to brief top submarine commanders on the sonar operations and maintenance course. Seattle, Washington is the first stop on the way to Sub Base Bangor which is located on the Hood Canal on the Olympic Peninsula. To get to the Sub Base from Seattle-Tacoma Airport, you must either drive over the Tacoma Narrows Bridge or take a ferry boat to Bremerton and drive the rest of the way. I took the ferry boat across Puget Sound. After the ferry boat docked, I drove toward Bangor and stopped on the way at the Bremerton Naval Shipyard to see the Battleship USS Missouri which was docked there at the time. Then I stopped at Poulsbo for the best salmon lunch I've ever had and arrived at the Sub Base a short time later. After showing my visitor's authorization pass, I was saluted through the main gate of Sub Base Bangor by U.S. Marine guards and drove to the new Trident Training Facility, (TriTraFac). At the new state-of-the-art training facility I met with my staff of instructors and then went on to the briefing room. A room full of U.S. Navy submarine officers sat in a semi circle room and looked down on me standing in the center of the amphitheatre stage. I began my presentation and for the next two hours fielded their questions about the training program. It was a stressful meeting with lots of questions, but a successful one and afterwards they invited me to have dinner with them at the Officers Club. Immediately after the briefing, the blue crew of the SSBN Ohio Submarine began a sonar operations course and their coffee mugs with their names on them were hung on the wall outside the classroom. To my surprise, one of the mugs had my name on it. I still treasure that mug today. Then I went to the Officers Club on base for dinner. As I looked out over the Olympic Mountains and the Hood Canal, I realized that I was a small part of a major weapons system that would defend our country for years to come and that in 30 years or so, when the SSBN Ohio Trident Submarine was almost ready for retirement, that's when I'd be almost ready to retire, too. I silently prayed that we would never have to launch the weapons of the SSBN Ohio Trident Submarine.

On my way home, I flew out of SeaTac airport and from the plane in the distance saw clouds of smoke and ash rising from the historic Mount St. Helens volcanic eruption.

A year later, just when I was beginning to feel like I was once again established in a career in ILS, I was asked to join the Technical Planning staff at FSD Headquarters in Bethesda, Maryland. This was seen as a career enhancing move and as a reward for the fine work done on the Trident Training Program. Customer praise for the program had reached the very highest executive levels in the division and the division president and his staff granted rotational assignments to top performers. I didn't want to go to Bethesda, Maryland but senior ILS management said they would take me back when the assignment was over and that since the offer came from the division president's office that I should not reject the offer.

Since I had joined FSD in 1973, I played a part in the following submarine systems events:

- 1973—Contract awards for the AN/BQQ-6 Trident sonar system and the Trident monitoring subsystem. I helped develop the monitoring subsystem trainer and course.
- 1974—Factory training and the first AN/BQQ-5 sonar system delivered to the SSN 688 Los Angeles. I conducted AN/BQQ-5 factory training.
- 1975-76—I helped to develop the curriculum and manuals for submarine crew training for both the fast attack submarines and the Trident ballistic missile submarines.
- 1977—The first AN/BQQ-5 sonar system went to sea that year and the contract was awarded for the 21B64. The first pre-production model was delivered to the Fleet Anti Submarine Warfare Training Center, Pacific, in San Diego, California. I helped develop a seven week operations and maintenance course and taught the operations part of the course to U.S. Navy submarine instructors.
- 1978-1981—I was promoted to Manager of Submarine Sonar Systems Training and over the next three years we conducted:
  - Trident Officers Indoctrination Courses,
  - Trident Initial Crew Training,

- Factory training courses,
- Navy civilian maintenance courses,
- The Sonar, Defensive Weapons, Command System Overview Course,
- Trident SSBN 726 Blue and Gold crew training,
- The Trident Sonar Operators Course, and
- We helped develop the proposal for the development and delivery of the LAMPS Mk III weapon system trainers—The Operational Flight Trainer, the Weapons Tactics Trainer, and the Avionics Maintenance Trainer. We won the contract.

The commissioning of the SSBN Ohio Submarine took place on November 11, 1981. My team and I received written praise in company newsletters and newspaper articles and most importantly, the U.S. Navy customer told our executive management that we had much to be proud of and had done a terrific job for the U.S. Navy.

SUMMARY LESSONS LEARNED

- **Sometime during your career, everything will look gloomy and you'll be depressed. Don't give up hope. Work harder, exercise, go on vacation.**

- **Just when you think there's no light at the end of the tunnel, something will happen to turn your career around. Whatever that is, it's the best option you have so you might as well accept it.**

- **Other people care about you, even people you don't know, and they want you to succeed. People will teach you what you need to know if you let them.**

- **Some people expect you to fail. Prove them wrong. I would never have thought that I could teach sonar to U.S. Navy submariners.**

5

FSD Headquarters

I left my job as Manager of Submarine Sonar Systems Training with great reluctance. I enjoyed being back in management and I was succeeding in the job. But, **to advance, you have to take chances and try different jobs that are offered.** The job at FSD Headquarters was that of a technical planner. I knew absolutely nothing about technical planning. The Director of Strategic Planning for FSD was responsible for the strategic direction of the business. The elements of technical planning included, but weren't limited to:

- Knowing the total financial picture of the division,
- Understanding the major contracts in the division and the technologies that distinguished IBM from its competitors, and
- Understanding what the customer needed and what changes were being planned at the highest levels of the Federal Government and particularly the Department of Defense.

Each FSD location had a technical planning department that had a strong connection to the Director of Strategic Planning at FSD Headquarters. Each location's General Manager reported in to the President of the Division on a regular basis and the Director of Strategic Planning attended most of those meetings. The FSD President frequently attended meetings at IBM's Corporate Headquarters in Armonk, New York and was also a Vice President of the IBM Corporation as well as President of the Federal Systems Division. I quickly found out that there was a lot to learn in the new position. It involved seeing the big picture of the business rather than performing on one piece of one or two major contracts. There were other major contracts at the other FSD locations like the Global Positioning System, the Space Shuttle, and the Federal Aviation Administration contract to modernize the nation's aircraft control systems. Every contract came to the attention of Strategic Planning at FSD Headquarters.

Technical and Systems Planning

My first assignment as a technical planner was to improve the organization control system, (OCS), which was a management information system that connected to financial, human resources, and other information technology systems. I became the "user chairman" of OCS and led a team of information systems people located at each FSD location who worked with me to improve the system. To improve the system I had to understand how the current system worked and where each and every department in FSD was located, who managed that department, how many people reported to that department, what the department was responsible for, and where the department "fit" in the organization. (i.e. where did the department report to and was it a first, second, third level or higher department?). This was not an easy task since FSD used a "matrix" organization approach for some contracts and a "functional" organization approach for other contracts. A matrix organization crossed organization lines and locations, and a functional organization typically was a vertical organization within one location. Staff functions like finance and contract administration, typically were functional organizations, but some were in a matrix organization. Many matrix organizations had departments that were geographically dispersed and not always located at the same FSD location. There were also "accounting use only" departments, and departments that had existed in the past but weren't purged from the system. As part of my development plan, I was sent to the Wharton School to study Organization Theory and to learn about different kinds of organization configurations and the systems that supported them. The course was very helpful and provided me with the idea that *how you organized a project or a business was a strategic decision. You could have a high number of technical experts, but if the organization wasn't supported by the right tools and systems, and if it wasn't designed correctly, the people in it would be at a disadvantage and work wouldn't flow smoothly.*

After achieving a base line for the FSD organization and isolating the unique reporting structures within it, I developed an OCS User Manual which became the specification for improving the system and its connections to other systems that the division relied on for accurate reporting. I worked closely with finance and accounting on the various kinds of reports that were required and learned to read financial statements and reports. I worked closely with location technical planners on population reports that were sent to human resources as well as site finance and accounting departments. And I worked closely with the information technology staff to schedule, track, and report on the progress of improvements made to the systems. And at the end of the project, I received a reward check for modernizing OCS.

My next assignment was to study the different kinds of contracts that the division was engaged in and generate a report on the trajectory of the government contracts we were pursuing as a division. Working closely with contract administrators at the locations, I found that there were many different kinds of contracts. The AN/BQQ-5 and AN/BQQ-6 contracts that I worked on were called "Cost Plus" contracts in that all costs of system development were reimbursed by the government contracting agent for the U.S. Navy and the 'plus' was the negotiated profit that the company would make on the deal. Profit incentives were added if performance on the contract resulted in less cost which usually meant delivering the product or service ahead of schedule. Another type of contract was called "Firm Fixed Price". Since more and more off-the shelf hardware and software could be purchased from other equipment manufacturers and used in some military contracts, the government implemented this type of contract which negotiated a firm fixed price for the product(s) or service(s). If the product or service was delivered on schedule, the company made a profit, but if the schedule was delayed, the company could lose money on the contract. Under cost plus or firm fixed price, contracts could be amended and changes negotiated. These so called engineering change proposals and engineering change orders were closely monitored as they could result in financial gains or losses. There were other types of contracts that involved engineering services, time and materials, fee for service, etc. A study of the contracts revealed that when some organizations in the division accepted a firm fixed price contract that involved developing software, there could be substantial schedule delays and financial losses because of the risk involved in the software development process. Additionally, managing subcontractors who did not deliver their products and services on time could also result in financial losses. Since more and more subcontractors were used in the firm fixed price contracts, the division had to rely on the technical skills possessed by the other companies which resulted in deterioration of the division's technical skill base. The study had many conclusions. As the division accepted more and more firm fixed price contracts, it was becoming a program manager of the contract for the government. Program managers had to be trained on managing subcontractors, and thorough risk management assessments were needed when bidding software development contracts. The study results and recommendations were well received and as a development assignment I was asked to accompany the Division President and Director of Strategic Planning to Armonk, N.Y. to attend a series of meetings with the IBM Director of Planning. We flew on a small propeller plane that seated six people. When the plane landed in White Plains, New York, we disembarked and were met by none other than the IBM senior executive that had ended the ASDD new product program I had worked on years before. He recognized me by name which impressed the FSD senior executives, (and me!). And, another stroke of luck! The IBM Director of Planning had worked with me at the IBM East Fishkill plant when I joined the company and had attended engineering education courses with me. He recognized me also which impressed the FSD executives. Altogether, it was a good trip and the FSD executives seemed glad they had brought me along.

After a year and a half at FSD Headquarters, I was offered a position as a Program Manager for the Light Airborne Multipurpose System, (LAMPS Mark III). I knew nothing about being a program manager but was sure that returning to Manassas meant more career options than staying at FSD Headquarters so I accepted the job.

Program Manager of Anti Submarine Warfare Systems

The LAMPS Mk III program involved IBM FSD computers and advanced signal processors to be installed on helicopters built by Sikorski with engines built by General Electric. The SH 60B Seahawk helicopter had a crew of three—a pilot who sat in the forward right hand seat and commanded the aircraft, an airborne tactical officer, (ATO), who monitored the tactical direction of the helicopter's mission and functioned as the co-pilot, and a Sensor Officer, (SO) who monitored radar and sonar acoustical data. The Seahawk helicopter was launched from a Frigate, (FFG), and was designed to detect any threat to the fleet. It was an anti submarine warfare system that electronically linked a shipboard systems crew with an airborne systems crew in order to localize and attack any threat to the fleet. Three trainers were built to support training for the SH 60B—The Operations Flight Trainer (OFT), the Weapons Tactical Trainer (WTT), and the Avionics Maintenance Trainer (AMT). As a program manager, I would manage the development of all three trainers.

A program manager in FSD meant that you managed a piece of a major contract or the entire contract with the Federal Government customer. The customer's primary connection to IBM was through the program manager. There were different kinds of program managers. A project program manager had the entire team of people that were working on the contract directly report to him or her. Usually, but not necessarily, this meant that all of the people on the contract were located at the same site. This approach ensured that the program manager had direct control over all of the people working on the contract. Another kind of program manager had no staff at all but controlled all of the funding for the contract as well as the customer interface. This kind of program manager had to rely on people in the organization who were not working directly for him or her and were often working on multiple contracts. In many cases, this meant that the people working on his contract could be located anywhere, at any location in FSD. People in between contracts could be tasked to work on this project for a time until they received an offer to work on a contract at their location. Unfortunately, I accepted a job as a program manager in this latter category. With no staff reporting to me I had to rely on FSD technical people throughout the company to support my contract. Surprisingly, they did.

The contract was complicated. It was a firm fixed price contract, had multiple subcontractors I had to depend on, and we were behind schedule and over cost when I took over. The contract had been modified several times and there were many engineering change proposals. My office was located in a building near Dulles Airport, but the people working on my contract were located in Owego, New York, so I had to commute often to Owego. That was also the location for LAMPS maintenance training. Owego had built hangars and a helicopter landing pad and it was common to see the Seahawks take off and land at the FSD site. I also traveled to General Electric in Lynn, Massachusetts for meetings with GE, Sikorsky, and the other helicopter subcontractors. I was able to baseline the contract and get it back on schedule and within costs. I was able to manage the subcontractors and meet delivery schedules. I won new and follow on business for FSD. The customer was pleased with my performance. And I was able to manage a remote staff that didn't report to me. I was in a key job and the customer identified me as a defense contractor who could manage this complex anti submarine warfare system contract. I traveled to Naval Air Station, North Island in San Diego to greet the first six Seahawk helicopters that were made operational at that time. A U.S. Marine guard saluted me at the gate and I recalled my days as an enlisted airman in the U.S. Air Force when I stood guard duty and saluted others at the gates of the air base. As I toured the LAMPs Training Center where the trainers had been installed, I looked at the student pilots and they seemed very young to me. In fact it was I that was getting older. I traveled back to Owego, New York and boarded a Seahawk helicopter that was being used in conjunction with the Aviation Maintenance Simulator to train U.S. Navy maintenance technicians. After taking pictures of the instructor and U.S. Navy trainees for a company newsletter, I returned to my office in Northern Virginia.

This was not the career I wanted. There were no opportunities for promotion, just a lot of aggravating technical, contractual, and managerial work that involved a lot of time spent away from home. I was told to be patient and that most top executives in the division had been program managers. They were right, but it didn't make me feel any better. I was ready to move on and wasn't sure that I wanted to be a top executive anyway if it meant too much time spent away from home.

Fortune intervened again. IBM Manassas needed someone who could manage a growing training organization and lead the effort to establish an interactive television program with the University of Maryland and who understood the missions of ASDD and CD well enough to develop learning resource centers and train their technical personnel. They offered me a promotion to accept the job and I did. My career had changed again and the training and development experience I had a decade earlier paid off.

SUMMARY LESSONS LEARNED

- **There are career limitations to being a "techie". It's a rewarding experience to be able to learn and teach technical topics and perform in a technical field, but your career opportunities may be limited to your field.**

- **Seeing the "big picture" from a headquarters staff perspective can be a tremendous learning experience. But don't stay too long at headquarters. There isn't a career there.**

- Don't be flattered into accepting a job that has serious limitations. If you don't like your job, don't be afraid to change careers and move on.

- Being a program manager in a defense oriented business is a fast way to become a top executive, if you're successful, if you like the job, and if you want to be a top executive.

6

Training and Development

In 1982, Personnel was now called Human Resources, (HR). They didn't want to give up the training and development mission, but the technical demands of the business called for a new type of leader for training and development—someone who knew what the business was all about, had technology skills, and had worked in a profit making function. Although the new position of Manager of Training and Development reported to human resources initially, it wasn't reporting there for very long. I didn't know it at the time, but the ILS technical function wanted me to manage the revenue producing "for-profit" ILS systems training business and was working behind the scenes to create another opportunity for me. The following year I was promoted back into ILS.

INTERACTIVE TELEVISION

Managers in human resources didn't know anything about applying technology to deliver education and training. At the beginning of the 1980's, programmed instruction, the IBM Personal Computer, and a host of new educational technologies were being introduced to the business. One of them was Interactive Television, (ITV). The University of Maryland had approached IBM in Manassas and offered to provide college courses to the IBM population via ITV. Studio classrooms at the University of Maryland would broadcast live classes and employees at Manassas who enrolled in the courses could see and hear the instructor and interact with the instructor and students in the class at the University through a telephone that was installed in the IBM classroom at each student's desk. A touch of a button on a panel in front of the student signaled to the instructor that the student had a question. To the best of my knowledge, IBM Manassas was the first major IBM facility to install and use ITV. Since the broadcast had a limitation of a fifty mile radius, a series of towers constructed by the University relayed the instructional broadcasts to Manassas. ITV was a big hit with IBM employees and employee enrollments at the University of Maryland surpassed enrollments at local Virginia colleges and universities. The program was funded through the tuition reimbursement program and was conducted part on and part off company time.

LEARNING RESOURCE CENTERS

The Components Division was renamed the General Technology Division, (GTD). They wanted to establish a Learning Resource Center and locate it in the plant library. The Learning Resource Center would allow employees to pursue learning skills through computer assisted instruction, audio-video self study, programmed instruction, and audio-tapes. After the Learning Resource Center was developed, many employees used the resources of the center to improve their skills.

IBM PERSONAL COMPUTER TRAINING

The IBM Personal Computer, (PC), was being introduced into the business areas in the early 1980's. Engineers and other employees didn't know how to use the IBM PC so we set up a PC Training Center, hired a few more instructors, and conducted training both on company and off company time. Up until this time, managers and technical professionals had to request data processing reports and obtain print outs of their requested reports from the site computing center. So called "dumb" terminals were connected to computers which could retrieve certain data for display at your desk. But people still had to fill out timecards by hand and submit them for data processing to tabulate labor reports. The IBM PC and new technologies promised to change all of that and eventually it did. Software application programs at the time were provided on 3.5" floppy discs and the monochrome display was in one color—green—except when the DOS symbol came up at the beginning of the PC session—that was in black and white.

CUSTOMER TRAINING

In 1983, ILS executive management offered me a promotion to a senior engineering position. Again I was stunned that I could be designated a senior engineer. But experience, in this case, was more important than an academic degree in engineering. All internal training and development for IBM employees as well as customer training was consolidated into one project. I became a second level manager and went to IBM Corporate Headquarters in Armonk, New York, to attend middle management school at the IBM Management Development Center. I had been in IBM 15 years and was now 42 years old. I thought that this was the highest management level that I would ever attain in business. Again, I was wrong.

I was an IBMer—a career manager with profit and loss responsibility. I had started my IBM career as a components division instructor, became a first line training manager in two years, then in succession, had jobs as a systems engineer product developer, a personnel recruiting and placement manager, an employee relations professional, a personnel researcher, a technical staff instructor in Federal Systems, an integrated logistics systems training manager, a technical planner, and a second level senior engineer training and customer education manager. I didn't know how to characterize my resume. I started to drop all of the jobs that weren't training and development related and began thinking of myself as a training professional who solved different training problems in different IBM divisions, but that definition of my "career" seemed very inadequate and didn't take into account all of the jobs I had or the technical experience I had gained in the submarine systems engineering field.

In Manassas, I managed four managers in four different departments and approximately 50 technical professionals plus interns, temporary employees, and administrative staff. One department was dedicated to internal IBM employee training and management development and three departments were dedicated to customer training support for all of FSD Manassas' contracts with the Federal Government. That included but wasn't limited to AN/BQQ-5, AN/BQQ-6, and Advanced Signal Processor (ASP), Training. In addition we addressed new business proposals for all contracts that involved training and development. I traveled to San Diego, California, Naval Air Station Millington in Tennessee, Newport, Rhode Island, and Sub Base Bangor, Washington.

In October, 1985, I published my first IBM technical report on Interactive Television and was invited to be a speaker at an IEEE professional conference in Williamsburg, Virginia. This was the first of many IBM technical reports that I would publish over the next decade, and the first of many national and international conferences where I would be invited as a speaker.

I found a career sponsor who was the Vice President and General Manager of Manassas. He supported the customer education and internal education programs I was managing and began to give me extra assignments to help him with the many community projects he had undertaken. Like most top IBM executives, he was involved in state and local politics and became friends with the Governor of Virginia. When he was asked why IBM was sourcing higher education degree programs from the University of Maryland, he asked me to attend a meeting of the Virginia senate subcommittee on education and provide them with an answer. I traveled to Richmond and described the University of Maryland's interactive television program to a committee of Virginia state senators. To my surprise a Richmond newspaper reporter attended the meeting and published the story in the newspaper. The news of my presentation went all the way to IBM Corporate Headquarters in Armonk, N.Y. It was not long after my presentation to the Virginia senate panel that state supported colleges and universities in Virginia like Virginia Polytechnic and State University and the University of Virginia began ITV programs of their own. IBM Manassas then began ITV programs with Virginia colleges and universities as well as the University of Maryland.

Just when I thought I had reached the pinnacle of my career, IBM Corporate Headquarters in Armonk announced that they would expand their Government Relations operations and select nineteen IBM professionals to be trained as lobbyists. With the support of my sponsor, I was selected to be the first IBM corporate lobbyist for IBM in the Commonwealth of Virginia. My career suddenly looked very different from the one I thought I had.

SUMMARY LESSONS LEARNED

- **Never lose contact with the people you've worked with and for in past assignments. Maintain a network of contacts and communicate with them often.**

- **You will work for managers that you don't like as well as for some that you do like. Either way, it's a temporary situation and you shouldn't let them interfere with your focus on your job.**

- **Community service tasks can lead your career in different directions.**

- **Having a corporate executive support your career is helpful but if that doesn't happen, be your own sponsor of your career.**

- **Write your resume in different ways and publish your achievements.**

7

Lobbyist

IBM Corporation had a Government Relations Office at 1801 K St. in Washington, D.C. The company did not contribute to political action committees, (PACs), but the company's positions became known because of its wealth, reputation, and international presence. Top level IBM executives participated on national committees and made personal contact with top legislative branch and executive branch government officials. But in the middle 1980's, the corporation realized that executive level personal contacts alone were insufficient to stay on top of the national and international issues that could impact IBM's business. A State and Local Government Department was established in the Corporate Government Relations Office whose mission was to develop a better understanding of state and local issues that could affect the company in the nineteen states where IBM had a major presence. State and local issues often became national issues. IBM put in place a tough screening process to select candidates that would be interviewed by Corporate Government Relations after endorsement by the top executive in the state. The people selected would need the knowledge, skills, and attributes that would enable them to communicate with elected officials, the press, and other executive level government relations lobbyists. Once selected, they would attend lengthy formal training sessions in public affairs conducted by IBM Corporate with the assistance of public relations external agencies and learn how to communicate IBM's position on corporate issues to elected officials at the "grass roots" and national level. The position title for government relations representatives was called "Program Manager of External Affairs". It was a high profile position that reported to the highest executive in the state and had a strong connection to IBM Corporate Government Relations. The top state executive in Virginia was my sponsor and mentor and because of the successful support I had provided him for state government issues in the past, I was recommended and selected as a candidate for the position.

WASHINGTON, D.C.

In early 1986, I left my job as a second level Manager in ILS, went to 1801 K St. in Washington, D.C., and joined a public affairs class of nineteen other IBM managers from around the U.S. who had been selected to represent IBM in their states as government relations representatives. Although I didn't know anything about being a lobbyist, my undergraduate degree in political science suddenly became very useful and enabled me to excel in the training session. In addition to studying the structure of the U.S. Federal, state, and local governments and the legislative process, the course covered all of IBM's public affairs issues in the U.S. and in the world. The class was taught by top IBM Corporate and Government Relations executives as well as by public affairs media consultants who provided training in how to deal with questions from the media and press. IBM's generous contributions to local communities and donations of surplus equipment and aid to schools were discussed by community relations executives. Representative from the corporate legal staff covered the legal requirements for lobbying elected officials. The formal training provided by Corporate was outstanding. Over the next several years, we would return to the IBM Corporate Government Relations Office many times, make many presentations, and receive briefings and updates from each other as well as from Corporate. In Manassas, I was given a nice window office and temporary offices at all of the IBM branch office locations in the state. Over the next few years I would meet and speak with many U.S. senators, U.S. Congressmen, U.S. Executive branch officials, Virginia governors, Virginia delegates, and Virginia state senators. I would travel and spend much time in the IBM Virginia branch offices in Arlington, Charlottesville, Norfolk, Roanoke, and Richmond. In 1987 I was promoted to an executive level in IBM. I was viewed as the registered lobbyist for IBM in the Commonwealth of Virginia.

RICHMOND, VIRGINIA

Since Richmond is the capital of Virginia, I was given an office in the high rise building overlooking the James River that served as the IBM branch office in the city. Every winter, beginning in January, the state government would convene at the state capital and I would spend the next three months in the capital attending committee meetings, attending receptions, and reviewing legislative proposals that could impact the company. When there were bills that required IBM to provide its opinion, I would register as a lobbyist and "educate" legislators on IBM's position and if there was a potential impact of the bill on IBM's business I would encourage legislators to consider the impact as well as consider alternatives to the legislation. When environmental issues arose, I briefed legislators on what IBM was doing to help clean up and protect the environment. I would give them tours of the Manassas plant so they could see for themselves what IBM was doing. When cross industry technology issues arose, I joined with lobbyists from other corporations to collectively voice our concerns and position. When I registered as a lobbyist I received a card which I showed to officials and at the end of the session filed lobbyist reports. This IBM was a very different world from the IBM that I had known.

Prior to and following the annual sessions of the Virginia legislature, I attended meetings of the Chamber of Commerce, state government events, and conferences around the state. I attended meetings of the legislative committee of the Chamber of Commerce in Northern Virginia and was able to meet with existing and prospective candidates for the Virginia house and senate. I met the Governor and Lieutenant Governor of Virginia, the state Attorney General, and many people in the executive branch of Virginia government. It was imperative that I meet and get to know as many elected officials as I could. I started by getting to know the local state delegates and senators where the IBM plants and branch offices were located and offered them tours of the IBM facilities, demonstrations of IBM products, and a briefing on what IBM was doing to help people in their district in Virginia. I developed a community relations inventory of all IBM programs in the state and authored a publication entitled "IBM in Virginia".

When the IBM state executive retired and a new state executive was named, I gained a new sponsor who enjoyed participating in public relations and community events. He asked me to invite the Governor of Virginia to visit the Manassas IBM plant. I was able to visit the Governor's mansion, meet with the governor, and obtain a seat on the Governors helicopter for the IBM state executive so that he and the governor could fly over Northern Virginia and get to know each other better. I led the effort to strategically orient our community relations initiatives and met with all of the major college and university presidents in the state. When IBM executives were appointed to governor's committees and task forces, I attended the meetings on their behalf and supported the governor's initiatives. For example, I attended meetings and provided support for the development of the Virginia Center for Innovative Technology. When a new governor was elected and a new IBM state executive appointed, I supported the new governor's initiatives to promote international education and attended meetings in Washington, D.C with high level government officials and corporate executives. I was invited to participate on The Southern Governors' Association Advisory Council on International Education and to assist in the development of a brochure on international competition and education. I was listed as a contributor to the publication and was invited to attend the Southern Governors Conference meeting in Charlotte, North Carolina.

I met nearly all of the U.S. congressmen and both U.S. senators in Virginia, many of whom sat on armed services committees in the house and senate. One congressman asked me to join his economic advisory council which I participated on for awhile. I attended conferences in Washington D.C. and met the Secretary of Defense, presidents of top corporations, U.S. Senators from other states and Governors from other states. Throughout 1987 and 1988 I was invited to attend many "black tie" occasions and the list of famous people that I met grew longer and longer. I was invited to participate on transportation committees and received letters from U.S. Senators and cabinet officials praising my participation on the committees. I even toured the FBI Academy where I gained great respect for the FBI and their mission, as well as their training methods.

Just when I started thinking of a career in government relations, the new President of what was now called the Federal Systems Company, (FSC), asked me to join the IBM FSC Technical Staff. I appealed to the IBM Manassas Vice President, General Manager, and leading executive in the state of Virginia to intercede on my behalf and keep me in my current job. But since he reported to the President of FSC, he advised me to accept the job. The job was made more acceptable when I was offered a position as Program Director on the technical staff and given yet another promotion. I was given an award for my performance a luncheon send off, and a picture of myself as a lobbyist in the state capital signed by the top executives at IBM Manassas and Corporate Government Relations with the inscription:

> A capital fellow!
> Thanks for knowing that
> "politics are almost as exciting as war,
> and quite as dangerous"
> Thanks for a job well done!

Although it might sound like I was an opportunist always looking for promotions and salary increases, I assure you that at age 47 with four children ready to enter college, there was a great incentive to assist them and start saving for retirement, so maybe being opportunistic wasn't a bad option at the time. In 1988, I gave up all of my offices in Virginia, introduced my replacement to my network of elected officials and contacts, hung up my tuxedo in the closet, and started to commute to Federal Systems Company Headquarters in Bethesda, Maryland once again.

SUMMARY LESSONS LEARNED

- **Following the lead of others is good practice in becoming a leader yourself. What may appear to be a step back could be a step forward.**

- **Never underestimate community relations, communications with the media and press, or government relations. But remember that they all have their own biases and interpretation of the truth.**

- **Attending too many black tie functions can cause you to gain weight.**

- **Meeting with high ranking government officials who are always in the limelight doesn't mean you'll be in the limelight, too.**

- **Being a lobbyist is not turning to the dark side. It is an expression of how American democracy works.**

8
Technical Staff

I quickly found out that IBM Federal Systems Company under the direction of its new president was focused on reducing costs, reducing investments, and reducing levels of management. They were concerned with the impact of these measures on the technical workforce. I was thrilled with the prospect of being a program director of technical vitality and reporting to the Director of Technology who reported to the Company President. But it wasn't long before my title was changed since other members of the technical staff also wanted to be program directors. At a time when management reductions were occurring throughout the company, it wouldn't look good for headquarters to be creating a number of program directors. I was very disappointed, but since there was no reduction in salary or assignment level, I got on with it. Senior managers on the technical staff included leaders in software engineering, systems engineering, integrated logistics engineering, and development engineering as well as senior technical leaders in other disciplines.

TECHNICAL VITALITY

My team and I developed a "Technical Vitality" program. This was a comprehensive review of all of the ingredients that went into the development of a world class technical workforce. It included but wasn't limited to:

- A review of the demographics of the technical labor force and recommendations for improvements,
- Tabulation of the number of patents, inventions, disclosures being generated and a review of licensable patents and inventions,
- The introduction of a technical vitality newsletter to share technical information across all company locations and with the rest of the corporation,

- An authors recognition program to encourage the development of technical publications,
- The formation of a corporate-wide council of senior technical staff members to look at current and future technologies and develop an inventory of independent research and development projects, and
- A focus on reducing overall training costs while prioritizing engineering education.

We were spending too much overhead in the wrong places. When I was tasked to implement the technical vitality program, I was authorized a small technical staff and given budget authority to take the actions necessary to reduce the overall training and development costs of the company, realign our investments, and focus the FSC sites on improving the technical skills and knowledge of the engineering workforce. The company started to reduce the total numbers of managers and levels of management at all of its locations. Management development programs were reduced along with non-technical education programs that were developmental in nature.

We established a senior technical staff composed of IBM fellows and distinguished engineers and scientists. This technical advisory board was chaired by the Director of Technology and the members of the board closely studied our independent research and development, (IRAD), projects. I attended the meetings of that board so as to better align engineering education programs with the strategic direction of the company. The technical advisory board also advised the company president on important technology issues.

A new technical vitality newsletter was formed and an author recognition program established. IBM still had a policy of no lay offs in those days. The managers removed from their jobs were retrained into technical leadership positions and whenever possible placed on contracts to generate revenue for the company.

I visited all of the FSC locations, formed a network of all of the education and training managers and met with them and their plant General Managers to track program realignments and cost reductions. In the first year, training and development budgets were reduced by two thirds and education staffs were cut in half. In the second year, further cost reductions and overhead staff reductions were undertaken.

Aspen Institute

Executive development was also being reduced and a review undertaken of out company executive training programs. I was sent to Aspen Institute in Aspen, Colorado, to evaluate and provide my opinion to executive management on their executive development programs. I liked Aspen, Colorado, and took my family there for a vacation in 1990.

Harvard University

IBM Corporate Headquarters was also interested in what all of the companies and divisions in the corporation were doing to reduce costs and were very pleased with the technical vitality programs implemented in FSC. They convened a one week seminar at Harvard University which I attended to discuss the FSC technical vitality program and learn of IBM's overall business situation and why training and education were being targeted for reduction. IBM was spending nearly a billion dollars on internal employee training and development programs at a time when the corporation was facing major market and technology challenges. Speakers from the Harvard University faculty provided a world wide perspective on the challenges yet to come.

When I got back from Harvard, I was invited to speak at the Defense Systems Management College, (DSMC), at Fort Belvoir, Virginia. I spoke to the class on the subject of competitiveness in the aerospace industry. DSMC is one of several government funded colleges and universities that trains civilian and military government program acquisition managers. My presentation was videotaped for future classes and well received.

By 1989, the technical vitality program was viewed as a successful program. All of the members of the FSC technical staff had contributed to its success. FSC started to look more and more at the possibility of expanding its government and defense business into state and local markets at home and with foreign governments abroad.

The Director of Marketing learned that I had studied Russian language at Penn State and later at American University. Since he spoke Russian also, he approached me in 1989 and asked if I would support a company marketing initiative to visit the IBM World Trade Headquarters in Paris, France, and develop and implement an IBM Technical Symposium to be conducted in Moscow, U.S.S.R. that Fall. He asked if I would give a presentation in Russian language to about 300 people designated to attend the conference from all of the Soviet Republics. I accepted his offer. For the next few months I was pre-occupied with visiting the main IBM education product facility in Atlanta, Georgia to get the latest information on IBM's newest educational technology products. I developed a report and presentation entitled "Education Technology in Industry" which would later be translated into Russian. We visited a local universities' Russian department and hired a Russian speaking professor to review my presentation and help me brush up on my language. With his help I was able to build the confidence that I could deliver the presentation in Russian. We arranged for distinguished speakers from the U.S., from France, from Great Britain, and from Sweden to attend the symposium and scheduled a meeting at IBM World Trade Headquarters in Paris, France in September, 1989.

PARIS, FRANCE

The last time I had visited Paris was in 1962 during the OAS-FLN war. It was nice to return to the city. IBM World Trade Headquarters was located in La Defense and we stayed at a nearby hotel.

Besides meeting with all of the symposium speakers, coordinating the schedule for presentations, and working on the logistics of getting into and out of the Soviet Union, we also wanted to develop a partnership with IBM World Trade in the event that we were able to attract new business opportunities. IBM had a branch office in Moscow and had done business in the Soviet Union for many years. FSC was a valued IBM partner because of its expertise in doing business with the U.S. and foreign governments, but this was clearly IBM World Trades market. After a week in Paris working on the symposium and learning about international business development processes and procedures, we were ready to fly behind the "iron curtain". We made arrangements to return from Moscow via Frankfurt, Germany and I thought this would be my last visit to Paris. But as fortune would have it, I returned to Paris once again on vacation in 1999. It's a place I will always love and remember.

Moscow, U.S.S.R.

My premonition from Penn State had come true. I was in the capital of the Soviet Union! From the time I was in elementary school in 1949 hiding under my desk in "duck and cover" nuclear attack exercises through the next four decades, the Russians were the enemy of the U.S. and therefore, my enemy. Any account of the major historic events of the last 50 years of the 20th century reinforced the story that the expansionist goals of the communist totalitarian Soviet Union was the cause of events like the Korean War, the Cold War, the Berlin Wall, the Cuban Missile Crisis, and the Vietnam War. The Soviet Union's formidable military and space achievements had built up an image in the West of a strong, monolithic empire. In 1989, going behind the "iron curtain" into the heart of the Soviet Union was an adventure that few were privileged to experience.

I was shocked and awed by what I saw in the ten days I stayed in Moscow. I stayed at the Ukraine Hotel, a Stalinist building with communist sickle and hammer stone décor. The hotel had a matron on each floor who asked for your key each time you left your room and asked you where you were going. I practiced my Russian often and became more comfortable talking with the Russian people. We had some time before the symposium started so I thought I'd wander the city and practice my Russian. Rather than take a taxi, I walked and took bus rides around the city. Moscow, in 1989, looked like a drab city that you might find in the third world. There was little traffic in the streets, the buildings were shabby and people lived in tenement housing reminiscent of public housing slums in the U.S. The skies were cloudy, the weather rainy, the people glum, the lines to get almost any item sold in city shops were long, and the looks people gave you were suspicious. There was no joy in Moscow.

But, to me, this was the city that was captured by the Mongols. Centuries later it was occupied by Napoleon. And another century and a half later, the city fought off the Nazi German army. Moscow and Russia had defeated them all. I wandered through the shops in the Arbat, the ancient Mongol marketplace. I went to the Kremlin to visit the Uspenski cathedral where Czars of Russia had been crowned for centuries. Russian orthodox icons covered the walls and pillars of the cathedral which had been turned into a museum and burial place for the czars of ancient Russia. I toured the Kremlin and saw the cannon of Napoleons armies lined up along the promenade. The Russia I studied in college became alive. I thought of all the books and poems I had read in Russian literature class by Tolstoy, Lermentov, Dostoevsky, Pasternak, Gorky, Gogol, Ahkmatova, Pushkin, and others. I saw the Bolshoi Theatre, famous for the Russian ballet and marveled at St. Basil's Cathedral. I shopped at the GUM department store and walked through Red Square where military May Day parades had been broadcast on western television for decades. I visited Lenin's tomb and the Russian WWII memorial where I saw young brides and grooms visit the memorial on their wedding day to leave the bride's flower bouquet. I saw where the American, John Reed, author of "*Ten Days That Shook the World*", was buried in the Kremlin Wall and thought about how my ten days in Moscow would shake my views of the Soviet Union. A short distance from the Kremlin was the National Hotel where Lenin had stayed and the infamous Dzerzhinski Square, home of the Lubyanka prison. The captured American U2 pilot, Gary Powers, spent some time there. I took a bus to Moscow State University in the hills around Moscow and from the campus of the university I looked out over the city. I visited the historic Novodovichy Convent and struggled to remember the lessons I learned from college texts on Russian history. I had studied Russian geography, history, literature, economics, and language and some of it was now recalled. Although you may dislike the government of the U.S.S.R., you can respect and admire the culture and history of the Russian people. I was glad I held a certificate in Russian Area Studies from Penn State.

Although Moscow had a long and interesting history, it lacked in good restaurants and hotels. Reservations in advance were required in order to eat at a hotel restaurant and the food was not particularly good. The hotel rooms weren't great, either. The musty Victorian age type rooms had high ceilings, the bathrooms lacked towels, and the beds were uncomfortable. I had the feeling the room was bugged because there were wires hanging from the ceiling fire extinguisher fixtures. In order to make a phone call you had to dial the operator, tell them the number you wished to call and then they would call you back hours later when they made the connection. There were no phone books or maps of Moscow. I found later that there were no printers or fax machines either as they constituted a "free press" of sorts that could be a threat to the government. Intourist was the official tourist center for visitors and one had the feeling that the police were everywhere, especially in the tourist offices.

We were met a few days later by the IBM Moscow branch manager who arranged bus service for us to the auditorium where the symposium was to be held. He spoke fluent Russian and he was an IBM'er who came from the Netherlands. The materials for the conference had been shipped directly to the branch office and surprisingly had arrived on time and had been delivered to the symposium auditorium.

We arrived early in the morning and the auditorium was already crowded with the participants. Many were distinguished scientists and engineers from the Soviet academies and universities. Some were professors and many were government officials. The symposium was sponsored by the Soviet Minister of Education and Culture. He welcomed the IBM speakers and guests and stayed for the entire symposium which lasted almost a week. The Russians had arranged for real time translation services. Each of the speakers spoke in their own languages—French, Swedish, English, etc. I was the only speaker who gave a presentation in Russian.

When it was my turn to speak, the translation services stopped and I nervously stepped up to the podium. I introduced myself, mentioned how happy I was to be in Moscow, and told the audience where I lived and that I was originally from Pittsburgh, Pennsylvania and had working class parents. I told them that I would try very hard to correctly speak their language and asked for their forgiveness in advance for any mistakes I might make. I then launched into my presentation. About half way through, I heard some laughter from the audience and thought I had mispronounced some words, or worse, said something stupid. After the presentation, the audience clapped enthusiastically which was unusual since the other speakers had not had a very enthusiastic response. I opened the floor to questions and answered all of their inquiries. When the question and answer session was over, a senior Russian official told me that the audience wasn't laughing at me and that I had done a very good job speaking their language which was difficult for westerners. He said that they had never heard their language spoken with a Pittsburgh, Pennsylvania accent before and everyone laughed. That evening I was invited to join some of the Russian symposium attendees at one of their favorite restaurants. A limo took me and some of the other speakers to a restaurant that had some of the best food I had tasted since being in Moscow and a floor show that featured costumed Russian folk dancers from all over the Soviet Union. After many vodka toasts, we were driven back to the hotel. I was treated very well and had enjoyed the symposium and restaurant. I had expressed an interest in visiting one of the schools for the gifted and talented in Moscow and the next day I was driven to Moscow School Number 67 where I was able to meet with students, teachers, and have lunch with them in the school cafeteria. I was very impressed with the school classes, their computer labs, and was surprised that some teachers and students spoke English. While in Moscow, we had also met with government officials and discussed several business proposals, but nothing came of those ventures.

Everywhere I went in Moscow, openness, (Glasnost), and restructuring, (Perestroika), were being discussed by every one. You could sense that change was coming but when it finally did come, it shocked the world and changed the course of history. I returned to the hotel and prepared to leave Moscow the next day and return home via Frankfurt, Germany.

One month after I left Germany, the Berlin Wall fell and the beginning of the end of the Soviet Union had begun. Twenty eight years earlier I had been in Germany one month before the Berlin Wall was built and I was there again one month before it was torn down. It went up and came down because people didn't want to live under communist totalitarian governments and many people had lost their lives trying to get to the West. The world was stunned when the Soviet Union ceased to exist a few years later. I felt that I had been a witness to the end of Soviet communism and one of the last businessmen to visit Moscow when it was still under a communist government.

The next year I attended a conference in Washington, D.C. and as part of the conference we were taken to the Russian Embassy. I had a chance to practice my language skills one more time. I didn't need an interpreter, and enjoyed the visit.

FSC Headquarters was now looking for new business and with funding support from the operational sites, I traveled to New Orleans and made a presentation in support of a business proposal to a three star U.S. Marine Corps General who had won the Congressional Medal of Honor. It was a great honor meeting him and making a presentation to him. However, we didn't win that bid.

I was able to propose and win a two year contract with the Defense Information Systems Agency, (DISA), to support the development of small defense contractors. Since Headquarters couldn't perform on contracts we transferred the contract to Gaithersburg.

At the University of Maryland, University College where I served on an advisory council, I was able to meet with a Japanese delegation. One of the members of the delegation mentioned that he was interested in IBM's experience in training and development and asked for a proposal on how IBM might help them develop an institute on the Izu Peninsula near Tokyo for use by five different Japanese corporations. With business development funding we developed and delivered the proposal but after that we never heard back from the requesting party. We contacted his office in Tokyo, but apparently they had no interest in pursuing the proposal further. *I learned that for international business a lot of proposals have to be developed before one finds new business.*

I traveled frequently to IBM corporate headquarters to help them develop the IBM Thornwood Education Center and a new "for profit" business called Skill Dynamics. The Gulf War broke out on one of my visits there in 1991.

I visited the National Defense University at Fort McNair in Washington D.C. to discuss new technical advances on the horizon in systems delivered education and distance learning. But, after my trip to the Soviet Union, everything seemed mundane and boring. I wanted to do something to support the war effort but that wasn't to be since the war was over in a few months.

I had just completed some workshops for the Environmental Protection Agency, (EPA), when I was tasked with supporting the National Aeronautics and Space Administration, (NASA), Headquarters in Washington, D.C.

NASA

The National Aeronautics and Space Administration had the same challenges that FSC and other government contractors faced in attracting, developing, and retaining engineers and scientists. As early as 1988 there was a national focus on accomplishing the national goals for education in order to develop a foundation for improving the nation's education problems. In 1991 NASA proposed the NASA-Industry Education Initiative and all of the corporations that had federal contracts with NASA were asked to participate in the initiative. Suddenly things seemed interesting again and I started to meet with NASA top leaders and other industry representatives from about 24 different defense and aerospace corporations. NASA contractors at that time included, but weren't limited to corporations like Boeing, General Electric, Grumman, Honeywell, Hughes, Lockheed Missiles and Space Systems Group, Martin Marietta, McDonnell Douglas Space Systems Company, Rockwell International, TRW Space and Defense Sector, Unisys, Loral, and Aerojet-General. I met with representatives from these and many other corporations and visited some of their facilities. NASA wanted to compile a report that summarized what those corporations were doing to support the national goals for education.

Aerojet-General Corporation

Sacramento is the state capital of California and home to Aerojet-General Corporation, a corporation that makes rocket engines for NASA and the Federal Government. I visited "Old Sacramento" and felt like I was back in western history when the pony express brought the mail from St. Louis, Missouri to this western outpost. At Aerojet-General, we held a meeting to start developing the outline and contents of the NASA report. After touring the Aerojet-General site and seeing the rocket test facilities, we went on to another meeting in southern California.

McDonnell-Douglas Corporation

Huntington Beach is just south of Los Angeles and home to a McDonnell-Douglas plant. It has facilities for training astronauts and I was able to walk through a mock up of the earth space station being built there at the time. It was a rare opportunity for me to walk through the space station and see how it was constructed as well as see the deep water tanks where astronauts experienced the weightlessness of being underwater and learned how to repair the space station. After several NASA sponsored meetings there, we returned to Los Angeles and flew back to Washington.

My name was added to yet another publication when the NASA-Industry Education Initiative Report was published in 1991.

Software Engineering Institute (SEI)

The Department of Defense was concerned about the quality of software and formed the Software Engineering Institute at Carnegie Mellon University in Pittsburgh, Pennsylvania. The Institute developed what was called the Software

Engineering Institute Capability Maturity Model, (SEI-CMM). It was a model that industry had to take seriously in order to be able to bid on future software development contracts with the Federal Government. The SEI would train assessors to determine the level of maturity that the organization had attained. To address this challenge, FSC tasked the Director of Technology to develop a software and systems engineering resource center to help the different FSC locations understand the new software standards and to adopt the recommended approach and model suggested by the Software Engineering Institute. We developed what was called the Software and Systems Resource Center, (SSRC).

SOFTWARE AND SYSTEMS RESOURCE CENTER (SSRC)

In the early 1990's, IBM was using the Professional Office System, (PROFS), for email and interoffice networking, but the Internet was developing its own momentum at the time. The SSRC would have the latest in information systems technologies and the best personal computers on the market. We started to store much of what our mission would be on the company's intranet, the Internet, and the World Wide Web. We moved to Rockville, Maryland. I published a few more technical reports during this period and was given two author recognition awards from IBM.

The Director of the SSRC had to be a software engineering executive and I would report to him along with program managers, systems engineering managers, and a technical staff. There were twelve people in my department alone and I had a substantial budget. It looked like my career had taken a step back since I would no longer be reporting to the FSC Director of Technology and would be turning over the technical vitality mission to others and picking up a systems engineering, program management, and software engineering training mission in support of the SEI-CMM. But I was placed on a bonus system in a technical function with an important mission, I was earning a six figure salary, and I viewed my career as having ended as I celebrated my 51st birthday and got ready for indoctrination into IBM's Quarter Century Club the following year. I viewed my role now as helping to develop, train, and mentor others. As it turned out, learning about the SEI-CMM and developing the SSRC provided me new knowledge and skills that led to another ten years of employment with other defense corporations, more international business trips, and promotion to higher level executive positions. *In a career sense, it was a case of one step back and two steps forward.*

SUMMARY LESSONS LEARNED

- As you approach the later stages of your career, a headquarters staff position can be beneficial, but your career might not end there.

- Being at the top of an organization provides you with visibility into new opportunities, new knowledge, and looks good on your resume.

- International business experience broadens your perspective, broadens your personal attributes, and opens your horizons to see the U.S. and the world from a different perspective than you'd get by limiting your career to domestic U.S. business. It is also requires a separate set of knowledge, skills, and attributes.

- Just when you think your career is over, taking a step back might mean taking two steps forward later. Don't give up before the game is over.

9

Quarter Century Club

On July 8, 1993, I celebrated my 25th anniversary with IBM. The Corporation was in deep financial and technical trouble at this time and a new CEO from outside of the corporation was selected to lead the company. Some spoke of breaking IBM into several smaller companies, but the new CEO opted to keep the corporation intact except for divesting itself of FSC. We were one of the more profitable divisions of IBM at the time, but the War in Iraq was over, the Soviet Union had dissolved, aside from the space shuttle there weren't any new major space programs on the horizon, and there were planned cut backs in government and defense spending. This triggered a wave of divestitures, mergers, and acquisitions in the defense industry that continues to this very day.

Being in the IBM Quarter Century Club had always been a milestone achievement. A certificate honoring 25 years of service, gifts, a check, a luncheon, and letters from the CEO and IBM top executives came with the occasion. A blue quarter century club seal was placed on your IBM badge and you entered a select group of senior IBM people. My membership didn't last long. Six months after I joined the club, IBM announced that it would sell the Federal Systems Company to Loral Corporation.

DIVESTITURE

The announcement hit IBM FSC like a shock wave. Letters and emails pored into the corporate office questioning why IBM was abandoning one of its most profitable company's and going against its stated practice of full employment. People were concerned over their benefits, pension status, jobs, salaries, and their future.

IBM announced that with the divestiture to Loral, most employees would be secure in their jobs. For those approaching retirement eligibility, the corporation would "bridge" individuals with more than 25 years of service to their 30th year anniversary or age 55, whichever came first and provide them with a traditional pension. I breathed a sigh of relief that all the years I spent with IBM were not in vain and at least I would have an IBM pension by the time I was 55. For those not qualified for the "bridge", grievances were filed and there was much resentment and sorrow.

No one knew anything about Loral Corporation and soon emails filled the network describing the Loral Corporation, its mission, its locations, and its management. It certainly wasn't IBM. There was a period from the end of 1993 to the first quarter of 1994 that was tough for most IBM FSC people to deal with. Everybody in FSC would become a Loral employee and all physical and plant assets would become Loral property. That was an individual and group identity crisis.

ACQUISITION

Few people knew what a divestiture meant and what was involved in the acquisition of FSC by Loral. We learned very quickly that we weren't IBM'ers anymore. It helped that Loral had grown by acquiring other company's and integrating them into their corporation. Loral management was skilled in the acquisition, consolidation, and merger process and quickly scheduled large "town hall" type meetings with employees and managers at the major FSC plant and lab sites. They welcomed everyone to Loral and explained the new corporation's management style, policies, practices, organization, and processes. The meetings, chaired by the Loral CEO, were helpful in providing employees with answers to their many questions and to help them deal with their fears and anxieties. During this period, a few thousand people decided to leave the company and some were given Loral's permission to transfer to other IBM commercial facilities.

MERGER

Space missions in FSC Houston were consolidated with space missions in Loral. The shipboard and defense systems mission was left in Manassas and connected to other similar missions in Loral and the defense systems missions in Owego were also connected with other similar Loral missions. The civil aviation, (FAA contract), mission in Rockville was placed directly under Loral management. The small FSC headquarters staff was integrated into Loral Corporate management. The SSRC and technical staff would now report to the Vice President of Technology in Loral, and the headquarters strategic planning and financial organizations were placed directly under Loral corporate management. Everyone was given a Loral badge, all stationary was changed to reflect the Loral Corporation, and by the second quarter of 1994, we all had become Loral employees. But the IBM FSC culture, practices, and management style lingered awhile longer.

IBM Summary

I thought I'd be at IBM FSC for my entire career, but I was wrong. After spending so many years thinking of myself as an IBM'er, I found myself in another corporation and it was a shock. I was depressed for months. I updated my resume because I thought that despite its assurances, Loral might lay us off. I reflected back on my years with IBM.

Through three of the corporation's divisions I had been an instructor, a training manager, a systems engineering product developer, a recruiting and placement manager, an employee relations professional, a personnel researcher, an instructional systems developer/instructor, a technical manual developer, an integrated logistics support engineering technical instructor and trainer expert, a submarine systems training manager, a technical planner, a program manager, a second level integrated logistics engineering manager, a corporate lobbyist, and a technical vitality manager at the headquarters level. I had worked and traveled to many IBM locations and defense contractor locations, military bases and federal government locations in the U.S. and I was to travel to many more in the next ten years. Appendix "A" provides a list of some of the locations visited in my career. To help guide you through the alphabet soup of abbreviations used in the defense industry, Appendix "B" provides a list of abbreviations used throughout this book.

I had worked on major Federal Government contract proposals—won some and lost some. And I had traveled on international business to Canada, France, and the former Soviet Union. How could I list all of that experience in a two page resume? I couldn't so I developed several versions of my resume.

SUMMARY LESSONS LEARNED

- Not even the largest, wealthiest, or the best of corporations can escape the pressures of historic, technological, social, and competitive market forces.

- Experience is gained by making mistakes. One must never cease to learn from ones own mistakes and the mistakes of others.

- You're never too old to change and adapt. Sometimes your own choices determine your career, and sometimes chance and other people's choices determine your career.

- No matter how secure you may feel in your job, remember that it is only a temporary condition. And if you spend no more than 2 or 3 years in a single job, you're probably on the right survival track. Customize your resume and develop several versions to address future job openings.

10

Loral

Loral Corporation had grown into a major defense contractor by acquiring parts of other defense corporations. Ford Aerospace, Goodyear Aerospace, Fairchild, Honeywell, Vought, IBM Federal Systems, and others were now part of Loral. The corporation chose to keep the operating divisions decentralized. Each had their own personnel policies and practices and corporate cultures. Loral's corporate headquarters in New York was kept small and the company only had a dozen or so corporate policies. The corporation had no centralized training and development organization and wasn't used to the scope of training and development that IBM FSC had supported. The SSRC was viewed as an asset because it would enable the Loral Corporation to achieve high levels of the SEI-CMM and therefore be able to bid on software development defense contracts. Consequently, Loral kept the SSRC, but didn't allocate a budget to support it. ***The entire operation was to be a cost center and recover its costs by selling its services to the other Loral divisions. If the total costs of the SSRC were not recovered, the center would be cut back until the costs it recovered equaled the costs of its operations and staff. If none of the other Loral divisions wanted to buy the services of the SSRC we would be out of business and out of a job.***

LORAL'S SSRC

For the next two years, the SSRC operated as a cost center and was able to support Loral divisions. We had negotiated a lower overhead rate than the operating divisions, therefore, Loral divisions could buy their services from the SSRC at a lower rate than that offered from the marketplace. Additionally, they would be funding internal Loral operations rather than paying for out company purchases and were gaining services, knowledge, and skills that would enable them to improve their software development processes.

The SSRC in Loral operated as a technical corporate institute and was organized to provide:

- Software and systems engineering process improvement consultation and conducting assessments of the organization's strengths and weaknesses in engineering process areas.
- A clearinghouse and web-based repository of technical information that was accessible only to Loral divisions and included process and standards documents, a software re-use repository, program management and engineering tools repository, databases of Loral experts in different technical areas and lessons learned from bids won and lost. Additionally, the SSRC provided for links to Internet resources such as the Software Engineering Institute and Defense Information Systems Agency.
- Leading edge technology teams that analyzed division tools and recommended best practices to improve the division's capabilities in software and systems engineering development, test, and integration.
- Software, Systems Engineering, Test and Integration, and Program Management training.
- Business development and contract support on requirements, cost, schedule, tools, methodologies, process and quality improvement, and reviews of existing contract program performance.

This was my first attempt at developing an institute-like center that used the emerging capabilities of the intranet and Internet. I led a senior experienced technical staff of systems engineering, software engineering, and program management instructors who understood life cycle product support from the initial phase of developing the proposal through the phases of system requirements analysis, systems engineering design, software engineering design, software development, systems integration and test, and logistics support after system delivery. They were able to provide consulting services and contract support services. They transferred in to the SSRC from all Loral divisions and locations and understood the different operating procedures and cultures of the Loral divisions. I was fortunate to be working with some of the best technical talent that Loral had to offer. We were able to recover more than our costs of operation during the first year which allowed us to expand our coverage to other Loral divisions the second year. Several Loral divisions achieved the highest levels of the SEI-CMM. Service to the Loral divisions involved extensive business travel but getting their respect and support was a major achievement for us.

Vought

One of the first trips I made was to Vought, a weapons and munitions manufacturer that was acquired by Loral. One of Voughts main sites was located between Dallas and Ft. Worth, Texas but they had other locations in the U.S. They developed deadly weapons systems and rockets used by the U.S. military. Systems and software engineering in support of weapons development was a major emphasis for them and they used the expertise of the SSRC to support their goals of improved quality and achievement of high levels of the SEI-CMM. I was given a tour of their facility and a briefing on the many weapons systems they developed for the military.

Librascope

Another early trip was taken to visit Librascope in Burbank, California. The company was formed during WWII and produced what was then called "Libra scopes" which were instruments that helped balance cargo on aircraft. After it was acquired by Loral, its mission was diversified to include biological and chemical detection equipment which was sold to the military. After taking a tour of the labs, I returned to Rockville, Maryland.

Goodyear Aerospace

One of our top systems engineers and I traveled to Akron, Ohio to meet with former Goodyear Aerospace leaders who now worked for Loral. They were working closely with Manassas on the development of shipboard and defense systems as well as working on foreign military sales and other defense products and services. They were located next to the airbase which was the home of the Goodyear Blimp. The facility was old and run down except for the lavishly appointed executive office suite. We worked closely with their software and systems engineering teams to evaluate the processes, tools, and methodologies they were using to support military contracts. We recommended improvements in different areas and they became a customer of the SSRC.

Loral, Salt Lake City

I traveled to Salt Lake City, Utah to meet with Loral management and brief them on the mission of the SSRC. I had never been to Salt Lake City and took some time to tour the city and see the Mormon Temple and the Great Salt Lake. Since they had little interest in SSRC products and services and since I was near the west coast, I then flew to Los Angeles, California to see if I could find other Loral customers.

Loral, Rancho San Margarita

Rancho San Margarita is just south of Los Angeles and I visited there to brief Loral management on the SSRC. There was also little interest in SSRC products and services at this location. I received a technical tour of the infrared sensor systems and weapons development contracts being worked on there and returned to Rockville, Maryland.

We were able to support many of the Loral divisions, but not all of them. I learned how difficult it was to sell internal overhead services to managers in corporate cultures who had never had much support in training and developing their people. I also learned that cost centers take a lot of management time, involve a lot of travel and salesmanship, and were short term focused. We were providing a valuable service to Loral, but we were also on a sinking ship without a budget or funding for improving our products and services. In our second year with Loral, we started to lose the technical talent that helped us at first succeed and then, after we had successfully supported the divisions in achieving higher SEI-CMM levels, we started to lose management support.

In 1996, Loral announced that it was selling its defense systems business and the SSRC to Lockheed Martin Corporation.

SUMMARY LESSONS LEARNED

- After being acquired by another corporation, it's best to try to understand as much about the new corporation as possible. Forget your past achievements.

- Try to avoid being placed in a cost center, but if you are, develop your marketing skills and update your resume.

- Strategic planning, understanding customer requirements, program management, and billable engineering services and products leads to profitability. But don't underestimate the value of other parts of the business.

- Creation of wealth is not the only reason a corporation is in business. They must also serve the higher purposes of their society.

11

Lockheed Martin

In 1996, we became a division of the Lockheed Martin Corporation which had been formed from a merger between Lockheed Corporation and Martin Marietta. It was interesting to see how people from IBM FSC who had become Loral employees referred to themselves. Most still considered themselves to be IBM professionals who happened to be sold to Loral and now found themselves in Lockheed Martin. *If you are forced into accepting too many corporate cultural identities in too short a period of time, you tend to fall back to the identity that's most familiar and comfortable.* We were all defense contractors, trying to survive the divestitures, mergers, and acquisitions that were shaking the industry from top to bottom.

Lockheed Martin didn't know what to make of the SSRC. We didn't easily fit into any corporate organization. They reported us to the Senior Vice President of Technology at Lockheed Martin's Headquarters in Bethesda, Maryland. The other Loral defense systems organizations continued to work under former Loral executive management which was invited to move into Lockheed Martin corporate offices in Bethesda, Maryland. But shortly after the acquisition, the former Loral executives formed a separate corporation called L3 and convinced Lockheed Martin to invest in that enterprise. Much of the former Loral defense systems business transferred into L3 and those components that didn't fit into L3 were merged into Lockheed Martin business units.

Lockheed Martin's CEO was involved in an aerospace venture to improve the quality of engineering education at colleges and universities in the U.S. He was supported by the Senior Vice President of Technology who, in turn, asked me to attend a conference of aerospace industry executives and deans of engineering from colleges and universities across the U.S. at Boeing in Seattle, Washington.

Boeing, Seattle, Washington

At Boeing, I had lunch with and spoke to the CEO of Boeing as well as the attendees at the conference. The intent of the conference was to come to agreement on what content improvements were necessary to reform engineering graduate and undergraduate education curricula. Most agreed that the world had changed and engineers needed a better grasp of business skills and concepts, social and leadership skills, and international business skills and knowledge. The concept of a "virtual engineer" was discussed. After the conference, I filed a report and toured the Boeing plant at Everett, Washington and the Boeing Museum. Following the conference, not much seemed to result from the effort to reform engineering education. Hopefully the recommendations discussed will be implemented in the future. When I returned later to Washington, D.C., I attended one additional meeting where the report on the recommendations of the aerospace industry executives was presented.

Sunnyvale

Lockheed Martin in Sunnyvale, California was located near a U.S. Air Force Base. I traveled there to meet with the manager of training and development and explain the mission of the SSRC. They had little interest in sourcing systems engineering, software engineering, or program management training from the SSRC. I was given a tour of the facility and saw satellites being built in clean room labs by engineers dressed in what looked like bunny rabbit pajamas. Lockheed Martin was a major contractor for the U.S. Air Force and NASA and built different kinds of satellites for them.

When I returned to Rockville, Maryland, I scheduled a meeting with the Lockheed Martin Director of Training and Development at Corporate Headquarters to explain the SSRC mission. I had known him when I was at IBM from prior University of Maryland events where we had served on advisory committees. He was interested in getting the SSRC training mission to report to him at Lockheed Martin Corporate and it seemed logical since the former director of Lockheed Aircraft's training and development organization now reported to him. He invited me to participate in a network of Lockheed Martin internal vice presidents, directors, and training managers from all U.S. locations. Their next annual conference was scheduled at Fort Worth, Texas at the former General Dynamics aircraft plant.

Fort Worth

My sense at the time was that the SSRC would not last very long in Lockheed Martin and the best survival tactic for me seemed to be to once again identify with the organization's internal training and development missions. I traveled to Fort Worth, Texas and attended the annual training and development conference. There I met vice presidents, directors, and managers of training from all of the Lockheed locations and learned the considerable scope of their missions and their accomplishments. The Skunk Works had an institute that focused on technical and business training. Corporate Headquarters sponsored three institutes that focused on management and executive development. Fort Worth's mission, (formerly General Dynamics), was building jet fighters not only for the U.S. Air Force, but for foreign governments. Their training mission was similar to the ILS training mission I had managed in Manassas. I was given a tour of the mile long aircraft manufacturing facility, the trainers used for pilot training, and got a glimpse at future fighter aircraft. Rather than sell the concept of the SSRC, I focused on learning as much as I could about Lockheed Martin. I received several invitations to visit different Lockheed Martin facilities and with support from Corporate, I scheduled visits to several Lockheed Martin locations.

Orlando

I traveled to Orlando, Florida to meet with the Lockheed Martin Corporate Director of Training and Development. I learned that his initiative to have me report to him in Bethesda was not approved by the Corporate Sr. Vice President of Human Resources. HR didn't want the training and development headquarters staff to grow and my salary at the time was too high for HR. I toured the Orlando facility where Lockheed Martin worked on contracts for the Apache Helicopter Program, Simulation Systems for the U.S. military, and the Tomahawk Missile Program among others. All was not lost—I went to Disneyworld to cheer up.

Denver

I had visited the IBM plant at Boulder, Colorado when I was employed at IBM and this was my first trip back to Denver in five years. Lockheed Martin's Aeronautics and Astronautics Division in Denver manufactured missiles for the military and for NASA. During my tour of the rocket facility, I noticed a rocket engine with Russian language signs and learned that the Russians were providing rocket engines to Lockheed Martin. Here was another reminder that the Cold War was over.

New Orleans

Another visit I made was to the Lockheed Martin facility in New Orleans. This facility was responsible for building the main fuel tank that was attached to the Space Shuttle. I toured the facility, was briefed on the training programs, and then toured old historic New Orleans before I traveled back to Rockville, Maryland.

I briefed the SSRC director on what I had learned from attending meetings, conferences, and touring Lockheed Martin facilities. The closest division in Lockheed Martin that would be interested in our products and services would be the former General Electric Aerospace division now called Management and Data Systems. But, they would be more interested, as corporate headquarters was, in only acquiring the courses, materials, and resources of the SSRC training mission. They had no interest in the other SSRC products or services. He then surprised me and said he'd received a call from a former IBM executive now at Lockheed Martin Headquarters requesting that I form a team and develop and deliver a distance learning study for the Indonesian Ministry of Education. I would be funded by corporate and work with an international business director from Gaithersburg on the project. After briefing my SSRC team and naming a temporary leader to take my place, I formed a new team and began work on a project that would take me to China, Southeast Asia, and Japan.

In July of 1996 I retired from IBM. I took my family on a vacation to San Antonio, Texas, visited the Alamo, walked along the Riverwalk, and went back to the two air bases where I had been stationed while in the U.S. Air Force—Lackland Air Force Base, in San Antonio, and Goodfellow Air Force Base in nearby

San Angelo, Texas. Both installations allowed me to drive onto the base(s) and reminisce about my time there. After my vacation, I prepared to visit Indonesia by getting malaria pills and inoculations for typhoid, tetanus, and hepatitis.

INDONESIA

The flight from Washington, D.C. to San Francisco and then on to Hong Kong seemed to take forever. I used the occasion to study Bahasa, the language of Indonesia and read up on the history and culture of the country. Upon arrival in Hong Kong, I stayed overnight at a hotel near the airport in Kowloon. After an excellent dinner in a nearby restaurant, I walked through a local park and watched elderly Chinese practice Tai Chi. I shopped in the downtown area and then returned to the hotel. The next day, I flew to Jakarta, the capital of Indonesia's 17,000 island nation.

Jakarta

Jakarta, Indonesia used to be called Batavia when it was colonized by the Dutch. The 5 star hotel where we stayed was an oasis in an area dotted by office buildings, slums, and mosques. Indonesia is the largest Muslim nation in the world and every morning I awoke to the call to prayer chants from the mosques surrounding the area. I checked in with the American Embassy to let them know of our business trip. We were driven everywhere in a government provided van with two guards provided by the Indonesian government. The next day we arrived at a suburban government complex that housed the offices of Pustekkom, the Center for Communication Technology of the Indonesian Ministry of Education and Culture. We were graciously welcomed, introduced to the Pustekkom staff, and presented with an overview of the Indonesian education system. We learned that the system involved grades 1-6 for primary education, grades 7-9 for secondary school and grades 10-12 for senior secondary school. Beyond the 12th grade students could apply for entry to colleges or universities. Since 1988, it was mandatory that Indonesian students attend nine years of basic education. There was a strong need to deliver education in areas of the country where teachers and education resources were not available. Currently, radio broadcasts and workbooks were being used. The Minister of Education and Culture had met with top Lockheed Martin executives who offered the study and they welcomed our interest in helping them examine the problems and recommend distance learning technology options. Indonesia was a major customer of Lockheed Martin and purchased military products and services from the corporation. I explained that the purpose of the Lockheed Martin study was to examine distance learning technologies and to recommend an approach that would enable teachers, students, and others in remote geographic areas to access education and learning resources. We made arrangements to tour schools in poor urban areas and in remote jungle areas of the islands. We planned to interview government officials, students, and teachers to get their views on interactive audio and radio technology, computer-based technologies, television and desktop video conferencing technologies, and mobile education resource centers. We would also examine electrification and telecommunications plans, the use of earth orbiting geostationary satellites, existing education infrastructure, and the development, production, and distribution of educational materials. They arranged for us to meet with Indonesian cabinet level officials before starting out for the remote areas of the country.

Prior to leaving Jakarta for remote areas, we met with top government officials from the Bureau of Planning, from Lapan, (the Indonesian space agency), and from the Indonesian office of management and budget. We met with officials and faculty of the University of Terbuka, the Indonesian open university that used interactive and broadcast television distance learning technology. We visited a public school in North Jakarta and two schools in very poor small towns on the outskirts of Jakarta. We took pictures, spoke with teachers, administrators, and students, and got an inside look at the facilities and technologies used at the schools. I spoke Bahasa as much as I could and found that they were delighted that I'd speak to them in their language. We were treated graciously wherever we went and the children smiled and asked us for our business cards. A few days later, we left by train and traveled to Bandung to tour vocational schools and meet with government and industry telecommunications planners.

Bandung

August is a hot, humid month in equatorial Indonesia and it was a relief to arrive in Bandung which was located in the highlands south and west of Jakarta. Dutch plantation owners had built homes in the area and the tree lined streets were a pleasant change from the hot busy city of Jakarta. The train ride took us past small towns where water buffalo pulled plows across rice paddies and at each railroad stop, vendors would run up to the train windows to sell their wares. I was reminded of India for some reason. I saw children swimming in brown river water. Run down card board and tin shacks along the train tracks served as homes for many poor people. But everyone was smiling and seemed happy.

In Bandung, I stayed at a hotel with a veranda overlooking the jungle. We were picked up in a government van and driven to a company called PT Telkom. We were joined by the education minister for Bandung who was educated in Pittsburgh, Pa., my home town. He described the run down conditions in schools, shortages of teachers, population increases, insufficient number of classrooms, and generally poor economic conditions. He thought that our ideas about mobile learning centers in vans might have merit. I had thought of the idea of using mobile vans equipped with computers, phones, and satellite connections from my experience with NASA's mobile schoolhouse which used trucks that traveled to inner city schools in the U.S. and helped educate students and teachers about NASA programs. When we arrived at PT Telkom we were given a tour of their interactive television center and vocational training center which looked like a military training camp. We learned that the Internet was just getting started in Indonesia and that the electrification plans would not immediately change the current conditions. Most remote villages lacked electricity. We thought that the mobile vans might be able to provide generators to help with electrification requirements for distance learning, telemedicine, and also serve as mobile schoolhouses.

Afterwards, we drove to a remote school in a mountainous region accessible only by dirt roads and located near a volcano. Some students looked ill. The classrooms were hot and dusty. A small radio in the corner of the room enabled them to access broadcasted lessons from Jakarta. When reception was poor, audio cassettes were substituted for the live broadcasts. Many of the teachers lacked formal teacher training and some were untrained community volunteers. Some students and teachers wore Muslim clothing, but it turned out that many of the Muslim children attended only the Muslim schools which were better equipped than the public schools. We returned to Jakarta by government van, stopped in a roadside restaurant to eat a burnt fish with rice on a banana leaf. We saw some of the smoking volcanoes in the region. Indonesia was a beautiful and dangerous country.

Back in Jakarta, I was invited to the home of the daughter of the Indonesian defense minister who was married to an American. The home was guarded by armed guards and surrounded by a fence. Inside, the floors were marble, the ceilings were high and the decorations beautiful. The den, next to the great room looked over a tropical garden and a large, stuffed Bengal tiger stared at me as I crossed the room into the dining hall. I was impressed. We proceeded to a restaurant in the old Dutch part of town and were entertained by a traditional Indonesian gamelan orchestra and waiters and waitresses in traditional Indonesian costume. The Indonesian meal was outstanding.

Over the weekend I was able to catch up on my notes, travel expense paperwork and visit local shops and parks. There was a concern for our safety the entire time I was in Jakarta and we were encouraged to travel in the government provided van with the two guards. Some of the neighborhoods we visited were described as very dangerous for westerners. They were impressed with our willingness to travel into the poor and remote areas and talk with the people. It was the 51st Anniversary of Indonesia's Independence Day and parades, flags, and speeches filled the TV stations. There was a strong military presence in Jakarta and I was told to avoid the Surabaya area, but I wandered over to Surabaya out of curiosity to satisfy my sense of adventure. I learned how to congratulate the people on their independence in Bahasa which impressed them and I got along just fine. On Sunday I shopped at a mall called Blok M and bought some items to take home. I returned to the hotel and packed for our trip to Yogyakarta.

Yogyakarta

We took an early morning flight on Garuda airlines and landed in Yogyakarta one hour later. Yogyakarta airport was a Japanese airbase during World War II and after the war was over, Indonesia took over all of the aircraft left by the Japanese and started their own airline industry. Yogyakarta is a major Indonesian education and cultural center. We were driven by van to the Pustekkom Radio Reproduction Center. We met with the local education minister and learned that satellite was not viewed as a viable option for distance learning because it was too expensive. Wireless telephone communications was a technology they were interested in learning more about. They produced hundreds of audio cassette courses every year for use throughout Indonesia. They reproduced the cassettes for distribution to the remote schools. We visited several remote schools which looked very similar to the schools we had visited in Bandung and Jakarta. One school was near the active volcano, Merapi.

After the visits and more meetings, we were driven on dusty roads through jungle terrain to Borobudur, an ancient Buddist Temple that is one of the wonders of the ancient world. The weather was clear and beautiful. I climbed the nine story high black volcanic stone pyramid to the very top. For centuries, Buddist monks would walk around the pyramid at each of the nine levels on a spiritual quest to eventually get to the top of the structure which represented heaven. On the top of the temple, I reached into one of the stone bells and touched Buddha's foot for good luck. It was an experience I shall always remember.

We flew back to Jakarta on a different airline but half way there had to return to the airport as the plane's cabin pressure fell, the temperature rose, and the cabin started to fill up with smoke. We transferred to another flight and landed safely in Jakarta one hour later. Was it touching Buddha's foot at Borobudur that helped me survive that flight? Because we were told of rioting and unrest in some of the areas we planned to visit, we decided to cancel our planned trips to Sulawesi, Sumatra, Irian Jaya, and Kalimantan and thought we had seen enough to put together a good study. Our guards told us that they were relieved since in some of the places we wanted to visit, they told us that they would be in more danger than us.

We met once more with the staff at Pustekkom and told them we'd return after the study was completed. We made arrangements to keep in contact with them and left the next day. We returned to Hong Kong, stayed overnight, and then flew back to the U.S. My first visit to Asia was another culture shock for me. I spent the next six months developing and writing the report and recommendations and reconstructing what I had learned from the trip.

We returned to Indonesia in 1997 via Hong Kong which was now in the process of being transferred to Red China. People in Hong Kong were leaving the city and many were nervous about the transition.

Back in Jakarta, Indonesia, we presented our findings. The Pustekkom staff were very pleased with our report and presentation. Before we left, they gave us gifts at a reception and dinner at an exotic restaurant located on two islands in a lake.

I will never forget the friendliness and warmth of the Indonesian people I met and those that I worked with on the study. Pustekkom invited me back to attend a conference in Bali the next year, but it was not to be. I flew back via Tokyo, Japan and stayed overnight in a hotel outside of Tokyo. While I didn't get a chance to tour the city, I marveled at Mt. Fuji, bought some Japanese souvenirs, and flew back to the U.S. the next day.

After completing the necessary travel paperwork from the trip, my wife and I went on vacation to Hawaii. When I returned from vacation the SSRC was being relocated to Gaithersburg, Maryland and pieces of our mission were beginning to be absorbed into Lockheed Martin business units. I was offered a promotion to Director of Training and Development in the Management and Data Systems (M&DS) business unit and accepted. Although I had been at an executive level in IBM and Loral, this was my first "Director" title. I turned the Indonesian project over to my team, said farewell to my staff at the SSRC, and relocated to M&DS. My office was in Fairfax, Virginia, but the main plants and labs for M&DS were in Valley Forge, Pennsylvania and I would spend several days a week there for the next two years.

VALLEY FORGE, PA.

The cultural environment at Management and Data Systems was still General Electric Aerospace even though they had been acquired by Lockheed Martin. Their policies, programs, and practices followed what they had learned from General Electric, (G.E.), and they viewed themselves as an organization that could probably teach Martin Marietta and Lockheed Martin a few things about the defense business. Lockheed Martin headquarters permitted M&DS to continue with their G.E. Aerospace heritage programs, culture, and General Electric management style. As long as M&DS wore the Lockheed Martin star pins, as long as their business stationary said Lockheed Martin, and as long as their profits went to Lockheed Martin, everything else was apparently endurable. Lockheed Martin understood that there was something to learn from every acquired corporation.

G.E. Aerospace had been an IBM FSC competitor in the submarine sonar systems business. As soon as M&DS leaders became aware that I had an IBM FSC background, the next two years became more and more interesting. It seemed to me as though many M&DS managers had a negative predisposition about IBM FSC. Many seemed envious of IBM and some just didn't like IBM. That feeling may have come from the intense competition between the two organizations over government contracts. M&DS leaders touted their training and development programs as the best in Lockheed Martin if not in the industry. They didn't seem to want me to change or modify their training programs. They expected me to learn about their heritage G.E. programs and administer them the way they always had been administered. In addition to my top secret clearance with the Department of Defense, I was granted top secret special compartmented information, (SCI), clearances. Consequently, I could have no further contact with Indonesia or any other foreign government. I was asked to attend the weekly meetings held by the president of the division at Valley Forge, Pa. and drove two hours to Philadelphia every week. Since the days at Valley Forge were long, I stayed overnight at least one night and many times for longer periods. Valley Forge M&DS management had some discomfort with the M&DS group in Fairfax, Virginia and the president tried to overcome that cultural quirk by traveling to Fairfax often. Nevertheless, senior management in M&DS viewed Valley Forge as the home base for the business unit and I was expected to spend more time there than in Fairfax. Initially I was supposed to report directly to the division president, but then he decided to report me to the director of strategic planning in Valley Forge. In the two years I spent with M&DS, my office in Northern Virginia was relocated four times. Local office changes didn't matter to me but I would never relocate to Valley Forge. The M&DS top executive in Northern Virginia was a former three star U.S. Air Force general who invited me to join his regional executive council. When he retired, his replacement came from the Central Intelligence Agency and my membership on the regional executive council continued. About a year or so later, I was asked to report to the vice president of human resources in Valley Forge. This reporting relationship would not last long.

I recall that my best times in M&DS were in managing a talented group of employees and managers, working with the process improvement team, working with the independent research and development team, and having a wonderful office on the 11th floor of a high rise building in Tyson's Corners, Virginia for six months. I didn't think that training and development should report to the vice president of human resources and was unhappy with the reporting relationship. In 1999, M&DS said they were consolidating their operations in human resources. Their idea of "consolidating operations" was to add management development to the training and development organization I was already managing, and they asked me to interview for the job I was already in because they were adding the management development mission. That made no sense to me. After receiving a positive performance appraisal and talking with the Vice President of HR and the President of M&DS, I was offered out company placement services and an early retirement pension. I accepted the offer and retired from Lockheed Martin on good terms.

I was provided with an office at a Tyson's Corners placement firm. I wrote several versions of my resume, and began searching for another job. I was now 58 years old and prospects for me landing another executive job at the salary I earned at Lockheed Martin didn't look good. But, I wasn't depressed. I was eager to move on to hopefully find a more positive work environment, find another defense contractor that would capitalize on my experience, and do something else that I might enjoy. I had visited many Lockheed Martin and defense contractor locations and had learned a great deal about the defense industry. Except for my experience with M&DS management, I liked Lockheed Martin. M&DS could have benefited and capitalized on my experience but they didn't. I was confident that another corporation would.

In my research at the job placement firm, I learned of an executive search firm in Northern Virginia. I called them, set up an interview, and asked them to call me if they ever had a client who was looking for someone like me. It didn't take long for them to call me. They had a client called TASC, Inc. who was looking for someone to establish a TASC Institute. They arranged a local pre screening interview for me with a TASC consultant that I grew to admire and respect and who I would work with over the next few years. I apparently did well in the interview session because I was invited to interview with the Vice President of Human Resources in Reading, Massachusetts. I wasn't enthusiastic about getting back into human resources, but I accepted the invitation, flew to Boston, took a cab to Reading, and successfully interviewed for the job. ***The position offered me more money than I was making at Lockheed Martin.*** The job would be located in Northern Virginia. It turned out that I would report to the vice president of human resources in Reading, Massachusetts for about six months before he resigned from TASC. I was very happy to be once again out of the Human Resources function. Before starting to work at TASC, we went on vacation to Paris, France, and celebrated the end of the 20th Century.

SUMMARY LESSONS LEARNED

- You will find good managers and poor managers wherever you work. Some may lack in the attributes you value. Some may lack in decision making skills. Your best approach is to find another job where you are valued for who you are and what you know.

- If you lose your job, make the best of it. Look forward with the same excitement and enthusiasm you had when you landed your first job.

- Never treat people disrespectfully. They'll remember your poor treatment of them and pay you back in kind if they get the chance.

- To survive as a defense contractor, you must have top security clearances.

- If offered early retirement, it's best to take it.

12

Litton Industries/TASC

TASC, Inc. was a division of Litton Industries. TASC, (The Analytic Sciences Corporation), was founded in Winchester, Massachusetts in 1966. It provided modeling, simulation, analysis, and evaluation of integrated navigation and guidance systems for the Trident Submarine Program, the Minuteman Missile Program and NASA's Space Shuttle. It evolved over time by acquiring ESD Corporation and WSI Corporation who were leading providers of weather information gathering systems. TASC was acquired by Primark Corporation, a global provider of financial, economic, and market research information in 1991. When I joined TASC in 1999, the company developed advanced information technology solutions for government and commercial clients in areas such as network and infrastructure security, systems engineering and modeling and simulation. Its customer base included the intelligence community, the Department of Defense, and other government agencies. In 1998, Litton Industries Inc. acquired TASC from Primark. TASC had major locations in Reading, Massachusetts, Colorado Springs, Colorado, Los Angeles, California, and Chantilly, Virginia.

Litton Industries headquarters was located in Woodland Hills, in Los Angeles, California. By the 1980's it became the world's leader in inertial navigation systems and in tactical radar warning systems and tactical command, control and communications systems. Litton acquired the Ingalls shipbuilding industry in Louisiana which built ships for the U.S. Navy and others. By 1999 Litton employed about 40, 000 people. In my first week at TASC, I traveled to Woodland Hills and was introduced to the network of training and development executives in the entire corporation. I told them of our plans to develop The TASC Institute and they invited me back to brief them on the progress and plans.

The TASC Institute

Only Reading, Massachusetts had originally wanted an institute and it established a web page which quickly fell into disuse. Information on the website was incorrect and employees ceased to visit the site. Other locations in the company offered classroom training and some functions had multiple E-learning contracts with vendors. In short, training was fragmented, decentralized, and uncoordinated. Frequent budget cuts at the different TASC locations diminished training and development programs. Each location was not easily able to access education program courses offered at any other site. Senior management decided to build an institute at the largest corporate headquarters location in Chantilly, Virginia, and hired me to plan and implement it. *I thought the time had come to develop a web based corporate institute. This meant that most, if not all of the training and development courses would be accessible on the company's intranet with a webpage on the Internet and World Wide Web.* I thought that TASC needed a web-based learning environment accessible also by TASC customers and business partners over the Internet and World Wide Web. I went to work developing the strategic plan for a web based corporate institute over the next few months.

The Strategic Plan

The TASC Institute would use computer-based training, video-conferencing, E-learning technologies, and traditional classroom training. Since TASC was recognized as one of the world's premier systems engineering and systems integration companies The TASC Institute developed a partnership with systems engineering and we jointly developed and sponsored a Certified Systems Engineering Program. Later this course would be sold to customers and business partners. The Institute would acquire an E-learning capability that would enable access to a complete on-line Microsoft Certified Systems Engineering Curriculum, a complete on-line Cisco Certified Network Administrator curriculum, and information technology training courses. To support the company's goal of acquiring high levels of the SEI-CMM, a software engineering program was developed that focused on new software technologies, processes, tools, and methodologies. An on line mentoring program was developed that had its own web page on the intranet. A distinguished technical lecture series featuring noted experts from academia, national laboratories, industry and government was implemented in partnership with a senior technical leader in one of the business units. Additionally, the institute would focus on project management and executive succession planning and development. A leading team of management development consultants for TASC had developed the framework for a management training program and The TASC Institute acquired that mission also. The institute was designed to shape the future of the company by developing strategic internal and external partnerships, implementing the Litton Leadership Development Program and shaping the corporate culture. The institutes classrooms and labs were to be located adjacent to research and development labs. Promising new technical leaders would be hired and placed directly into the institute. They would be provided with advanced technical training, introduced to research and development projects, and later placed in key positions in the company. The program was named the TASC Technology Leadership Development Program and was widely praised by management.

As the Director of the TASC Institute, I reported to the Vice President of Administrative Services one level below the company president. I was asked to join the President's Executive Team. I served on research and development and systems engineering committees and was directly involved in the company's mission. The following year, Litton corporate executives called the institute a "best practice" and the Corporate Vice President of Training and Development visited Chantilly, Virginia to learn more about the institute and to discuss using it as a model for a corporate university. He was interested in the process used to develop the institute as well as some of the difficulties encountered in obtaining management and executive support for the institute.

I described the process used to develop the web based corporate institute as follows:

- The commitment of the company's executive management was obtained first and regular briefings for the TASC executive management team scheduled.
- A web based survey was developed to assess training requirements at each of the company's locations in the U.S. and at the TASC location in the United Kingdom. I visited all TASC locations in the U.S. and met with their top management to get their ideas on how a TASC Institute could help them.

- Once the requirements were known and analyzed, various models and institute designs were presented to executive management and one design was adopted. The design involved establishment of one centralized institute at the major, headquarters location in Chantilly, Virginia, and an E-learning capability that would enable all of the sites to access technical courses at any time and at any place. The mission of the institute would encompass:

    - Management training, the Litton Leadership Development Program, and Succession Planning,
    - Tuition reimbursement and college and university relations,
    - Compliance, Harassment, and Ethics training,
    - Business courses, lecture series, and new employee orientation,
    - Information technology training,
    - Software, and systems engineering education, and the
    - Technology Leadership Program.

- An inventory was taken of all of the training courses, training facilities, budgets and staff. The results of the inventory and requirements assessment were presented to executive management and after that, all training budgets, resources, facilities, and a small staff was authorized for the Director of The TASC Institute.

- Duplicate facilities, staff, and courses at all locations were eliminated and one E-learning contract that would support all locations replaced the many E-learning contracts in the company. Cost savings were immediate and substantial. With support from a consultant, an on line mentoring program was developed and implemented.

- A communications program was implemented, brochures and catalogs were made available, and the web site revitalized and showcased by the company in competitive bids and to customers. Video labs, research and development labs, and learning centers were co-located near classrooms in the new building and the institute was chartered to train new, high potential technical hires prior to their being placed in the organization.

- A compact disc, (CD), was developed for New Employee Orientation that standardized the program for all company locations and provided new employees at remote organizations with links to the company's intranet for additional resources and contacts. Film clips on the CD introduced new employees to executives and senior leaders throughout the

company who gave brief introductions about their organizations and missions.
- The company's intranet was analyzed for capacity and robustness in providing web casts, video streaming, and high quality E-learning courseware. It was determined that video streaming was not an essential requirement at the time.
- In the year 2000, a training facility was constructed in a separate building at the headquarters location with "The TASC Institute" prominently displayed on the exterior of the building.

The TASC Institute would have its own logo, brand name, and web page on the company's intranet as well as the Internet and World Wide Web. The Corporate Vice President of Training and Development was impressed with the progress we had made in the short time I had been with TASC. He invited me to attend a Litton Industries Conference that would be held at a prominent hotel in West Palm Beach, Florida that summer.

WEST PALM BEACH, FLORIDA

The Litton Industries Conference lasted a week and featured top corporate speakers, tours of historic West Palm Beach museums, and the opportunity to once again meet with the training and development executives I had met in Los Angeles just a year ago. The Corporate Vice President of Training and Development reported to the Sr. Vice President of Human Resources and I could sense that HR once again would be taking over the training and development mission. Discussions with my immediate manager, following the conference validated my suspicions.

Upon returning to Chantilly, Virginia, I had made up my mind to seek employment in another corporation. This was no easy decision since I was now 59 years old and my long term career prospects were not good. I updated my resume with an executive search firm and asked for their help to acquire another job and soon afterwards, I was contacted. They had found another client who was interested in my experience and background and who also wanted to develop a corporate institute.

I successfully interviewed for the position with the Senior Vice President for Organization Development, the CEO of Veridian, and several presidents of the Veridian divisions. I was offered a job as the future Director of what would become the Veridian Institute. We went on vacation to Italy, and when we returned, I found out that Litton Industries, (and TASC), had been acquired by Northrop Grumman. I speculated whether I should have stayed with TASC and continued my career with Northrop Grumman, but decided that there was a great probability that The TASC Institute would not survive the acquisition, that human resources would be consolidated in Northrop Grumman, and that my career in that corporation would be of a short duration. As it turned out, I believe that I was right in moving on. I decided that I could develop a better web based corporate institute for Veridian based on my recent experience with TASC and the lessons learned from developing The TASC Institute.

SUMMARY LESSONS LEARNED

- Use executive search firms to find a job. They don't charge you and collect their fees from their clients.

- Using a logo and brand name a web based corporate institute distinguishes itself from the rest of the corporation and elevates it to a position of prominence.

- Weigh all of your options carefully before you decide to move on.

- It is better to leave a corporation on your terms rather than the corporation's terms. Leaving a success story behind builds your reputation.

- Your family and personal life always takes top priority in any decision.

13

Veridian

Veridian was a leading provider of information based systems, integrated solutions, and services. It specialized in providing mission-critical national security programs for the intelligence community, the Department of Defense, law enforcement, and other U.S. government agencies. Veridian had grown by acquiring other companies. It had facilities in Ann Arbor, Michigan, Fairfax, Virginia, Roslyn, Virginia, Chantilly, Virginia, Los Angeles, California, and its headquarters was in Arlington, Virginia. It had famous astronauts on its board of directors and its CEO was actively involved in Aspen Institute programs.

Veridian was similar to TASC in that there was no systematic training program in place for the entire organization. The operating divisions of Veridian had differing company cultures in that they were acquired by the parent company and so had different approaches to developing human resources and conducting business. The CEO of Veridian wanted a single integrated company and was committed to developing a Veridian Institute at the corporate level.

THE VERIDIAN INSTITUTE

Since I had years of experience managing and leading training and development organizations in major defense corporations like IBM, Loral, and Lockheed Martin and had developed the SSRC and The TASC Institute I was ready to launch into developing the Veridian Institute, however, some major obstacles confronted me. First, I reported to the Sr. Vice President of Organization Development who reported in turn to the CEO. He had his own ideas about a corporate institute and believed in doing a lot of research into how other companies had developed their institutes and universities before deciding the course of action. Second, many senior leaders in the company were not enthusiastic about a centralized corporate institute and wondered how it could address the training needs of their unique cultures. Each business unit had its own human resource department which operated independently from the rest of the company. Finally, I had to meet with all of the senior leaders, describe my role, understand their business areas, and convince them that the corporate institute was a good idea. This process would take almost a full year.

Training coordinators were scattered around the corporate business units reporting to different organizations. One division had an "institute" of sorts which served primarily as a customer training department for that one division. Managers in the divisions were opposed to losing their overhead training budgets to a central institute. With the CEO's support, I explained to them at numerous meetings that the corporate institute would not be designed to perpetuate the existing disparate cultures and ways of doing business, but would be a top down catalyst for serving their organizations training and development needs and integrating its culture into a single Veridian corporate culture.

The Veridian Institute would be developed primarily as a cultural change agent and provider of innovative, high quality learning solutions in the common areas of business development, project management, technical training, compliance, and leadership development. Moreover, it would be a web based corporate institute providing all employees and managers with access to its services.

At the corporate level, a senior human resource professional was hired by the Sr. Vice President of Organization Development to integrate the various personnel policies, practices, and programs into a corporate-wide human resources organization. That individual left the company in six months or so and was replaced by a second senior human resource professional. The Veridian Institute would not report to a fragmented HR function. Corporate HR had its own integration and acceptance problems in the company.

During the first year, a review of the latest technologies regarding simulation, distance learning, and web based instruction was undertaken. The applicable technologies were demonstrated at exhibition fairs conducted by the company. ***In one simulation, a web based corporate institute was simulated on line and employees could experience a "virtual reality" walk through an on line institute.*** Virtual reality on line institutes were in the experimental stages at the time. Simulations of business decision games were reviewed for applicability to the new institute. I tracked the research and development that would dramatically improve the Internet over the next few years and decided that the days of traditional classroom training were nearing their end. *In the future, chat rooms, simulations, interactive video, and E-learning would be the preferred way for corporations to deliver instruction and web based corporate institutes would replace traditional training departments.*

After a year of studies, reviews, requirements assessments, visits to all of the Veridian locations, and financial options analysis, one model emerged as the choice of executive management. The model included the following provisions:

- The Veridian Institute would have no separate training facility. Existing conference rooms and classrooms were to be used wherever they were located if they were needed.

- The preferred model of a "virtual" institute was adopted. E-learning would dominate the offerings of the institute. But a centralized project management training program would also be developed with the support of an external vendor. This program, too, could be delivered on line. But the time it would take to modify the courseware and the cost of procuring it from a vendor was prohibitive. The company opted to have the project management training program delivered by a vendor and Veridian instructor via traditional classroom training. In retrospect, while the vendor provided courses were very successful and received outstanding student feedback, an on line project management approach would have worked and resulted in lower overall costs.

- The software and systems engineering training programs required by the SEI-CMM, would remain decentralized and not become the mission of the institute.

- The institute director would participate on several major systems and software engineering internal committees and chair the program management council.

- An intranet website and external Internet website was developed. The intranet website focused on internal programs and the Internet website focused on customer education.

- Access to information technology and compliance E-learning courses, a registration process, course catalog, and other company resources would be from the institute's intranet website. Corporate legal counsel played an important role in selecting the compliance E-learning courses and helping to modify them.

- New employee orientation programs would remain in decentralized human resources departments at the division level which would report to the presidents of each division. The institute Director would continue to report to the Senior Vice President of Organization Development. That position was one level below the CEO and the Director of the Veridian Institute would have open and frequent access to the CEO.
- Customers could be provided with training courses under existing and new contracts but each contract program manager would determine how and if that would be done.
- A leadership academy would be developed by the institute. The leadership academy would focus on developing management training programs for new managers, mid-level managers, and executive managers. With the help of external vendors, on line tools were provided to prepare managers for workshop sessions and performance assessment tools were made available that would assist in succession planning.
- The primary role of the institute was to act as a cultural change agent for the company and help the CEO integrate the various company cultures into a Veridian Corporate identity.
- An extensive communications plan including brochures, web announcements, videotapes, and corporate senior leadership meetings led by the CEO were launched. Seminars were conducted at management leadership meetings.
- The corporate institute staff would consist of a registrar, E-learning and technical instructor, a program management instructor, and an instructor/developer for management development and the leadership academy. These four individuals played a key role in the success of the Veridian Institute.

From its inception, the Veridian Institute was viewed as a web based "virtual" institute and 80-90% of its products and services were web based. Veridian customers could view the products and services offered by the institute on the Internet. Customer training courses were planned for web-based access and sales and the institute was referenced in bids and proposals to assist in obtaining new business. The institute also had a robust intranet website accessible by all employees and managers. The intranet website provided a catalog of all training courses offered, hundreds of E-learning information technology courses, on line compliance and ethics courses, registration procedures, policies, practices, and links to other performance support information. Also on the web page of the Veridian

Institute, the CEO of Veridian provided a video web cast to all employees supporting the institute with his personal endorsement of its products and services.

The web-based institute was launched in 2001 and fit very well into the corporate strategy. The culture started to change and people started to work across business unit functions and organizations and began to identify themselves with Veridian rather than with their heritage organizations. As the business improved and grew, the institute received strong support from senior management throughout the corporation. The following year, Veridian would acquire Signal Corporation.

THE PENTAGON, SEPTEMBER 11, 2001

I traveled to Veridian's Headquarters in Arlington, Virginia at least once a week and had a temporary office there. The 12 story building located at South Hayes Street housed the Rand Corporation and the Pentagon City Mall. I usually took the Orange line metro to Roslyn and then transferred to the Blue line which took me directly to Pentagon City. It was my habit to arrive early. The view from my office window looked out over the Pentagon. It looked to be about a half a mile away.

On September 11th I was on the phone talking to a representative of the Office of Management and Budget when I heard and felt a huge explosion. The whole building shook violently. I got off the phone and people on my floor started running to the elevators and exits. The Vice President of Communications was waving his arms and shouting at people to get out of the building. Some people were crying and many employees were in a state of subdued panic. I started for the stairs but decided to take the elevator instead since it looked safe. I didn't know what had happened and thought that maybe a bomb had exploded in our building. I went to the Pentagon Mall on the bottom floor and saw that the shops were closing and people were evacuating the Mall. I went outside to South Hayes Street and saw a stream of people walking across the Pentagon South Parking Lot. A huge black cloud of smoke rose up from the Pentagon into a clear blue sky. I knew then that something terrible had happened at the Pentagon.

My cell phone wasn't working so I went back into the Mall to call my wife and stood in a long line of people making phone calls from a public pay phone. After telling her I was okay, I learned that a plane had crashed into the Pentagon and television reports indicated that planes had crashed into the World Trade Center in New York, too. Any thoughts of an accident were ruled out. I went down to catch the Metro back to Vienna and was told it was not operating. Buses had been called by Metro to pick up people and transport them to the Ballston Metro stop in Virginia. I left the Metro Station and returned to South Hayes Street. It was a beautiful Autumn day and I was awe struck watching the ominous, ugly, black cloud of smoke still rising against that clear blue sky. I waited in a long line and eventually got aboard a bus, but it was stalled in traffic for hours. I met and spoke to a civilian retired Lt. Colonel in the Department of the Army who had just come from the Pentagon. He was in shock and was trying to get home. He said his office was down the hall from where a plane had struck the Pentagon. He said he was concerned about leaving his briefcase on his desk as he crawled out of the building in the smoke filled halls of the Pentagon. He said it was the worst experience he had had since he was in Vietnam. I tried to call my wife again on my cell phone and was very lucky to get through as most of the cell phone connections were down. She said that one of the World Trade Center buildings had collapsed. I told the people on the bus and they gasped in disbelief. We knew then, that it was a terrorist attack on the U.S. After a couple of hours had passed, I got off the bus. We had gone only about a block from where I got on the bus at Pentagon City. I started walking back to the metro stop. On the way, I saw many men and women in uniform gathering by cars with open doors and listening to the news reports on the radios. It reminded me of what Pearl Harbor must have been like. Ambulances were everywhere and stunned people were still streaming across South Hayes Street from the Pentagon. The Pentagon parking lots were now blocked off and no one could go toward the Pentagon. When I arrived back at the metro station, the metro had started running again. It didn't stop at the Pentagon like it usually did and I changed trains in Roslyn, rode back to Vienna, and drove home.

It took me a long time to adjust to what I had just experienced. It was hard for me to imagine an attack on the Pentagon. When I arrived home and watched the twin towers of the World Trade Center in New York City collapse after planes had purposely crashed into them killing thousands of innocent people, I was depressed, shocked, and very angry. If they would have taken 60 year olds in the military, I would have re-enlisted right there and then. But that was not an option for me. I returned to work the next day and learned that one Veridian employee was on the flight that crashed into the Pentagon.

A few weeks later, my wife and I went to New York City on a business trip. We took the subway and got off at Wall Street. Conductors on the subway wore masks as we approached the vicinity of the World Trade Center. We put on masks, too, and walked over to what was now called ground zero. We saw and smelled the smoking, burning, ruins of the World Trade Center buildings. First aid workers, firemen, police, and national guardsmen patrolled the area. Trucks sprayed the streets with water to wash away dust and debris. We learned that nearly 10,000 children lost a parent on that horrible day. Pictures were posted on bulleting boards by the Trinity Church of those that were missing. Saddened and angry, we wished that everyone could have seen what we saw on that day so they could remember that awful tragedy that impacted so many families.

THE LAST YEAR

In the summer of 2002 I attended a training director's conference in Las Vegas, Nevada and later that fall attended an Aspen Institute course at Wye River, Maryland. But after 9-1-1, nothing seemed right. I went through the motions of launching and managing the Veridian Institute in 2002, but my heart was no longer in it. I felt that the world had changed again in a significant way and that the nation had to call upon its young people in the military once more to defend our country. I decided to retire for good when I turned 62 the following year. People said I was too young to retire but I knew better. The CEO encouraged me to stay. But my mind was made up. In early 2003, I was given a small send off, a token retirement gift, a bonus, and left Veridian and the defense industry for good. Several months later, Veridian was acquired by General Dynamics. I never found out what happened to The Veridian Institute. My guess is that it was dissolved into the acquiring company.

SUMMARY LESSONS LEARNED

- Web based corporate institutes are a wave of the future that will give corporations who establish them a competitive edge in the marketplace.

- A corporation's culture will determine the kind of corporate institute it will need. The term "corporate institute" is preferable to the term "corporate university" because it more accurately describes the specialized mission of a corporation.

- A corporation that doesn't invest in the development of its people lacks leadership attributes and values that will impact its business.

- Corporate institutes are like sand castles. The first strong tide of organization change may wash them away.

- Someday you will have to leave the work world. Do it gracefully.

14

Epilogue

In ancient times when people lived in caves and thatched straw huts, men looked to other men to fashion weapons they could use to hunt, feed themselves and their families, and to defend themselves and their families against other men. These stone club and flint arrow makers were the first defense contractors. In ancient Egypt men learned that new weapons technology like chariots pulled by horses, armor, and hardened metal swords and spears could help them better defend their nation, their culture, and their families against invaders. The Romans viewed weapons of war in a larger sense and trained their armies and navy in maneuver and tactics, equipped them with wooden machines of war, and recruited men who could build roads, bridges, aqueducts, and stone fortresses. During the middle ages, men specialized in providing armies and navies with the latest armor, long bows, crossbows, and castles. **Down through the ages, through the 18th, 19th, and 20th centuries men have relied on defense contractors to equip them with weapons to defend themselves. And now in the 21st century this tradition continues and defense contractors are still serving the national interest.**

I felt like I had played a small part in a centuries old occupation and a small part in American history. Over the last three decades I had:

- Supported U.S. Army, Navy, Air Force, and Marine Corps proposals and contracts. Most of my contract defense work was in support of the U.S. Navy Submarine Service, the historic development of new classes of submarines and the development of a new anti submarine warfare helicopter and the computer systems that enabled it to function.

- Supported proposals and contracts for the intelligence community and visited the National Reconnaissance Office, and the National Imagery and Mapping Agency as well as other government agencies.

- Traveled to Canada, France, the former Soviet Union, Indonesia, Japan, and Hong Kong, China in order to develop and conduct international business.
- Visited National Aeronautic and Space Administration headquarters and NASA labs in Maryland and Virginia. I toured space shuttle support facilities in Houston, Huntington Beach, and New Orleans.
- Worked in Federal Aviation Administration facilities, postal facilities and worked with the Department of Labor and the Environmental Protection Agency.
- Been aboard nuclear submarines and helicopters and visited many U.S. military installations.
- Helped train thousands of defense industry professionals, managers, and corporate leaders as well as customers.
- Developed two corporate web based institutes, a software and systems engineering resource center, and been on the forefront of the introduction of new educational technologies.
- Traveled on business to more than thirty four major cities in the U.S. and nine major cities in foreign countries.

Since I was a child hiding under my desk at school with other children fearing nuclear war as adults did in the 1940's and 1950's, I have always known that there are people in the world that do not like us and will attack us if we are weak and unprepared. When "Sputnik" was launched, our enemy was the Soviet Union. Today, the enemy is terrorists from the Middle East. Our children, our country, and our nation relies on defense contractors to build the best airplanes, the best submarines, the best ships, the best guns, the best electronic sensors and the best equipment that will allow our young men and women in the military to protect themselves, protect our families, protect our nation, and preserve our way of life. Defense contractors train our soldiers, sailors, airmen, and marines on how to use those weapons to defend themselves in warfare. Defense contractors today serve side by side with military volunteers on ships at sea, on submarines, on bombers, in jet fighters, on helicopters, and other weapons systems. You can find them on airbases, naval bases, and army forts here in the U.S. as well as in tent encampments in Iraq, in Afghanistan, and in countries around the globe. Defense contractors also provide services to help astronauts explore space and intelligence officials to use sophisticated equipment to accomplish their missions. Defense contractors support space agency officials, civil aviation officials, public health officials, postal officials, state and local governments, and other public service organizations to make our country a better place to live.

We should all be grateful for the men and women of our military who put their lives on the line to defend the freedoms we enjoy and their partners, the defense contractors, who serve with them. I'm proud to have been a small part of this story and to have served as a defense contractor for most of my working career.

Retirement gives one a chance to reflect on ones life. I've learned that there are many ways a person can serve their country. I've learned that I've played a very small part in the working world. I've learned that my spouse and children helped me throughout my career and together we survived the daily struggles of living. I've learned that you don't succeed solely on your own and others have helped you to succeed. I've learned to appreciate the work of others pursuing their chosen vocations. The lessons learned summaries at the end of each chapter don't convey the full extent of everything I've learned from three decades in the defense business. In this short journey we make between two great eons of darkness—the darkness before we were born and the darkness after we're gone—I've learned that each individual is greater than the occupation they pursue and the infinite spark that shines in us all assures everyone a unique place in the history of mankind.

These memoirs are my attempt to share my experience with future generations so that they may know that others had to struggle to make a living and survive just as they will have to do. If the lessons learned in this book helps them or if they can retrieve one small nugget of wisdom from these lessons learned, then the book is worth the effort.

APPENDIX A

List of Some U.S. Locations Visited

IBM Locations	Military Bases	Contractor Sites	Government Sites
Poughkeepsie, N.Y.	USN, Wash, D.C.	Unisys, Fairfax, Va.	DISA, Wash, D.C.
E. Fishkill, N.Y.	U.S. Army, Ft. Monmouth, N.J	Hughes Aircraft, L.A., California	U.S. Post Office, New York City
Manassas, Va.	U.S. Army, Ft. Monroe, Va.	General Electric. Lynn, Mass.	Naval Sea Systems, Arlington, Va.
Owego, N.Y.	USN Sub Base, San Diego, Calif.	General Dynamics, Groton, Conn.	NASA HQ, Wash. D.C.
Gaithersburg, Md.	USN Sub Base, Bangor, Wash.	Aerojet-General, Sacramento, Ca.	NASA, Goddard, Maryland
Burlington, Vt.	USMC Base, New Orleans, La.	McDonnell-Douglas, L.A., Ca.	NASA, Langley, Virginia
Yorktown Heights, N.Y.	NAS North Island, San Diego, Ca.	Rockwell, Int'l, L.A., Calif.	Defense Systems Management College, Arl., Va.
Armonk, N.Y.	NAS Millington, Memphis, Tenn.	Boeing, Seattle, Wash.	National Defense University, Washington, D.C.
White Plains, N.Y.	Naval War College, New London, Conn.	Vought Systems, Ft. Worth, Texas	FBI Academy, Quantico, Va.
Houston, Texas	Ft. McNair, Wash. D.C.	Librascope, Burbank, Ca.	NRO, Fairfax, Va.

IBM Locations	Military Bases	Contractor Sites	Government Sites
Denver, Co.	Ft. Belvoir, Arlington, Va.	Loral, Rancho San Margarita, Ca.	NIMA, Fairfax, Va.
Los Gatos, Ca.	USN Base, Bremerton, Wash.	Goodyear Aerospace, Akron, Ohio	Russian Embassy, Washington, D.C
San Jose, Ca.	USAF Base, Langley, Va.	Loral, Salt Lake City, Utah	FAA, Leesburg, Va.
Raleigh, N.C.	USMC Base, Quantico, Va.	Lockheed Martin, Sunnyvale, Ca.	NUSC, New London, Conn.
Rochester, Minn.	Fleet ASW Training Ctr, San Diego, Ca.	Lockheed Martin, Denver, Co.	NASA Manned Spacecraft Center, Houston, Texas
Chicago, Ill.	USAF Base, Sunnyvale, Ca.	General Dynamics, Ft.Worth, Texas	SEI, Pittsburgh, Pa.
Thornwood, N.Y.	USMA, West Point, N.Y.	Lockheed Martin, Bethesda, Md.	EPA, Washington, D.C.
Endicott, N.Y.	USNA, Annapolis, Md.	Lockheed Martin, Valley Forge, Pa.	National Aca. of Science, Wash. DC
Lexington, KY.	USAF Academy, Co.Springs, Co.	Lockheed Martin, Orlando, Fla.	Dept. of Labor, Washington D.C.

* Also worked at TASC, Veridian, and visited Aerospace Corporation, Mitre, etc.

APPENDIX B

List of Some Abbreviations

AMT—Avionics Maintenance Trainer
AOCR—Advanced Optical Character Reader
ASDD—Advanced Systems Development Division
ASP—Advanced Signal Processor
ASW—Anti Submarine Warfare
ATO—Airborne Tactical Officer

CAI—Computer Assisted Instruction
CCS E&I—Command and Control Subsystem Engineering and Integration
CD—Compact disc
CLIN—Contract Line Item
CMM—Capability Maturity Model

DID—Data Item Descriptions
DISA—Defense Information Systems Agency
DOD—Department of Defense
DSMC—Defense Systems Management College

E—Learning—Instruction delivered electronically over computer networks
EPA—Environmental Protection Agency

FAA—Federal Aviation Administration
FBI—Federal Bureau of Investigation
FSC—Federal Systems Company
FSD—Federal Systems Division

GE—General Electric Corporation
GPS—Global Positioning System

IBM—International Business Machines Corporation
IRAD—Independent Research and Development
ILS—Integrated Logistics Support
Internet—A subset of the World Wide Web accessed by Internet Service Providers
Intranet—An organizations internal network that can connect to the Internet
ITV—Interactive Television

LAMPS—Light Airborne Multi Purpose System

NAB—National Alliance of Businessmen
NASA—National Aeronautics and Space Administration
NEO—New Employee Orientation
NUSC—Naval Undersea Systems Center
NVCC—Northern Virginia Community College

OAC—Objective Assignment Chart
OCS—Organization Control System
OFT—Operational Flight Trainer

PAC—Political Action Contribution
PC—Personal Computer
PPP—Personnel Performance Profiles
PROFS—Professional Office System
Pustekomm—Indonesian Center for Communication Technology

SCI—Special Compartmented Information
SEI—Software Engineering Institute
SH60B—Designation for Seahawk Helicopter
SLT—Solid Logic Technology
SO—Sensor Operator
SSRC—Software Systems Resource Center

TASC—The Analytic Sciences Corporation
TLA—Training Level Assignments
TSOT—Trident Sonar Operator Trainer
TRADOC—U.S. Army Training and Doctrine Center
TTF—Trident Training Facility

WWW—World Wide Web—a global network made up of other networks

About the Author

T. H. Henning had multiple careers over the 35 years he spent with International Business Machines Corporation, Loral Corporation, Lockheed Martin Corporation, Litton Industries/ TASC, and Veridian Corporation. As a defense contractor he worked on military and government contracts for much of his career and also developed two web based corporate institutes. He is a veteran of the U.S. Air Force and received his Bachelors and Masters degrees from The Pennsylvania State University. He and his wife Cheryl reside in Northern Virginia.

Index

A

Acquisition 46, 57, 65, 83
Advanced Signal Processor 30, 36, 97
Aerojet-General 53, 95
American University 11, 19, 46
AN/BQQ-5 16, 20, 21, 22, 23, 25, 29, 36
AN/BQQ-6 16, 23, 25, 29, 36
AN/UYK-7 21
Anti Submarine Warfare 20, 22, 25, 30, 31, 92, 97
AOCR 14, 15, 97
Armonk, N.Y. 5, 30, 37, 95
ASDD 10, 11, 12, 13, 17, 30, 32, 97
Aspen Institute 46, 84, 90
Atlanta, Ga. 47

B

Bandung 70, 71, 72
Bangor, Washington 23, 24, 36
Barbizon Plaza Hotel 5
Berlin Wall, 48
Boeing 53, 65, 66, 95
Borobudur 73
Bromont, Canada 8, 9

C

Carnegie Mellon University 53
CCS E&I 97
Central Intelligence Agency 2, 75
CEO 56, 57, 65, 66, 83, 84, 85, 87, 88, 90
CLIN 97
Components Division 3, 4, 5, 7, 8, 9, 10, 11, 12, 17, 35, 36

Cost Centers 63
Customer Training 35, 36, 85, 87

D

Defense Contractors 18, 51, 65, 92, 93, 94
Defense Information Systems Agency 51, 61, 97
Defense Systems Management College 46, 95, 97
Denver, Colorado 96
Department of Defense xi, 14, 15, 27, 53, 75, 78, 84, 97
Department of Labor 9, 10, 93
Divestiture xii, 56, 57

E

East Fishkill, N.Y. 3
E-Learning 79, 81, 82, 86, 87
Environmental Protection Agency 52, 93, 97

F

Fairchild 60
FBI Academy 42, 95
Federal Aviation Administration 27, 93, 97
Fleet Anti Submarine Warfare Training Center, Pacific 22, 25
Fort Monmouth 16
Fort Monroe 16
Fort Worth 67
FSC 42, 45, 46, 47, 51, 52, 54, 56, 57, 58, 60, 65, 74, 97
FSD 12, 13, 14, 16, 17, 25, 27, 28, 30, 31, 36, 97

G

Gaithersburg, Md. 95
General Dynamics xii, 67, 90, 95, 96
General Electric 30, 31, 53, 68, 74, 95, 97
Global Positioning System 27, 97
Goodfellow AFB, Texas 1, 69
Goodyear Aerospace 60, 62, 96
Government Relations 37, 39, 40, 42, 43
Gulf War 52

H

Hampton Institute 16
Harvard University 46
Honeywell 53, 60
Hong Kong 69, 73, 93

I

IBM xii, 2, 3, 4, 5, 7, 8, 9, 10, 11, 12, 13, 14, 15, 16, 17, 19, 20, 21, 22, 23, 27, 30, 31, 32, 34, 35, 36, 37, 39, 40, 41, 42, 44, 45, 46, 47, 49, 50, 52, 54, 56, 57, 58, 60, 65, 66, 68, 74, 84, 95, 98
IEEE 36
Indonesia xii, 69, 70, 71, 72, 73, 75, 93
Integrated Logistics Support 17, 19, 58, 98
ITV 34, 37, 98

J

Jakarta, Indonesia 69, 73
Japan 68, 74, 93

K

Kerhonksen, N.Y. 4
Kirknewton, Scotland 2

L

Lackland AFB, Texas 1, 68
Lamps Mk III 26, 30
Lexington, Ky. 96
Librascope 62, 95
Litton Industries xii, 78, 82, 83

Lobbyist 37, 39, 40, 41, 42, 43, 58
Lockheed Martin Corporation 63, 65
Loral xii, 53, 56, 57, 58, 60, 61, 62, 63, 65, 74, 84, 96

M

Management and Data Systems 68, 74
Manassas, Va. 95
McDonnell Douglas Corporation 53
Merger 57, 65
Monitoring Subsystem 16, 25
Montgomery College 14
Moscow State University 49
Moscow, U.S.S.R. 47, 48
Mount St. Helens 25

N

NASA 14, 52, 53, 66, 68, 71, 78, 93, 95, 96, 98
National Alliance of Business 9, 98
National Defense University 52, 95
Naval Air Station Millington 36
Naval Air Station North Island 31
Naval War College 23, 95
NEO 4, 98
New Orleans, La. 95
Newport, Rhode Island 23, 24, 36
Northern Virginia Community College 9, 98
Northrop Grumman Corporation xii, 83

O

OAC 98
OCS 28, 29, 98
OD45519 16
Operational Flight Trainer 26, 98
Orlando, Fla. 96
Owego, N.Y. 95

P

Paris, France 47, 76
Penn State University 2

Pentagon xii, 14, 88, 89, 90
Personnel 4, 5, 7, 8, 11, 12, 13, 16, 17, 20, 24, 32, 34, 36, 58, 60, 85, 98
Personnel Performance Profiles 16, 20, 98
Pittsburgh, Pa. 1, 71, 96
Point Loma, Ca. 22
Postal Systems 15
Poughkeepsie, N.Y. 4, 10, 95
Pustekkom 69, 72, 73

Q
Quarter Century Club 54, 56

R
Rancho San Margarita, Ca. 96
Reading, Massachusetts 76, 78, 79
Richmond, Virginia 40

S
Safeguard 14, 15
Salt Lake City, Utah 63, 96
San Diego, Ca. 95, 96
Seahawk Helicopter 30, 31, 32, 98
Seattle, Washington 24, 65, 66
SH60B 98
Signal Corporation 88
Sikorski 30
Software Engineering Institute 53, 54, 61, 98
Sonar Operator Trainer, 21B64 20
Southern Governors Association 42
Space Shuttle 27, 56, 68, 78, 93
SSBN Ohio Submarine 24, 26
SSN Los Angeles 25
SSN Pintado 22
SSRC 54, 58, 60, 61, 62, 63, 65, 66, 67, 68, 74, 84, 98
Subcontractors 29, 31
Sunnyvale, Ca. 96
Systems Integration 18, 21, 61, 79

T
TASC Institute 76, 78, 79, 80, 81, 82, 83, 84
TASC, Inc. xii, 76, 78
Technical Planning 25, 27
Technical Vitality 44, 45, 46, 54, 58
TRADOC 16, 98
Trainers xi, 17, 20, 21, 23, 26, 30, 32, 67
Training Level Assignment 16, 20, 98
Trident Sonar Operator Trainer 17, 23, 98
Trident Training Facility 24, 98

U
U.S. Air Force Academy 1
U.S. Naval Academy 23
U.S.S. Missouri 24
University of Maryland 2, 32, 34, 35, 37, 52, 66

V
Valley Forge, Pa. 74, 75, 96
Veridian xii, 83, 84, 85, 86, 87, 88, 90, 96
Veridian Institute 83, 84, 85, 86, 87, 88, 90
Vought 60, 62, 95

W
Weapons Tactics Trainer 26
Web Based Corporate Institute xiii, 79, 80, 83, 85, 86, 91
West Palm Beach, Fla. 82
Wharton School 28
World Trade Center, N.Y. 89, 90
World Trade Headquarters 47
World Wide Web 54, 79, 82, 98

Y
Yogyakarta 72

978-0-595-36326-1
0-595-36326-1